Visa Denied:

How Anti-Arab Visa Policies
Destroy US Exports, Jobs and Higher Education

by

Grant F. Smith
Special Regional Research by Tanya Cariina Hsu

Published by the Institute for Research: Middle Eastern Policy
Calvert Station
PO Box 32041
Washington, DC 20007

First published in 2006 by the Institute for Research: Middle Eastern Policy

7   9   10   8   6
Copyright © Institute for Research: Middle Eastern Policy
All Rights Reserved

Library of Congress Cataloging-in-Publication Data

Smith, Grant F.
Visa denied : how anti-Arab visa policies destroy US exports, jobs and higher education / Grant
F. Smith ; special regional research by Tanya Cariina Hsu.
p. cm.
ISBN 0-9764437-6-7 (alk. paper)
1. United States--Foreign economic relations--Arab countries. 2. Arab countries--Foreign
economic relations--United States. 3. Arab countries--Relations--United States. 4. United States--
Relations--Arab countries. 5. Exchange of persons programs--Government policy--United States.
6. Cultural relations--Government policy--United States. 7. United States--Foreign relations--
2001- I. Hsu, Tanya C. II. Title.
HF1456.5.A6S64 2007
337.73017'4927--dc22
2006035540

Table of Contents

1.0 Executive Summary 7
2.0 Free Travel and Free Trade: The US National Interest 9
3.0 The Trade Consequences of US Visa Barriers 19
    Affected Industries 21
    Key US State Stakeholders 23
4.0 Turning Away the World's Highest-Spending Tourists 25
5.0 Cutting America's Link to Tomorrow's Leaders 29
    Fixing the Fulbright 33
6.0 Country-Level Damage Assessment 37
    United Arab Emirates 37
        The Dubai Ports World Debacle 38
        Politics vs. National Security Concerns 39
        DPW Analysis and Lessons Learned 41
    Saudi Arabia 45
        2005: A Year of Missed Opportunities 46
    Egypt 50
    Kuwait 51
    Algeria 53
    Qatar 54
    Iraq 55
7.0 Conclusions: Restoring Visitors and Trade 57
Appendix - Opportunity Cost Methodology 59
    Travel and Tourism 59
    Arab Students 59
    Arab Market Imports from the US 59
    Direct and Indirect Manufacturing-Related US Job Creation 59
Appendix – Best Case US Share of Arab Import Market by Country 61
Appendix – Actual US Share of Arab Import Market by Country 62
Appendix - Arab Student Enrollment in US Higher Education by Country of Origin 63
Appendix - Total Direct US Manufacturing Jobs Generated by Exports to the Arab Market (By Industry) 64
Appendix - Direct US Manufacturing Jobs Generated by Exports to the Arab Market (By Origin of Movement) 65
Appendix - Direct and Indirect US Jobs Generated by Manufactures Exports to the Arab Market (By Origin of Movement) 67
Appendix - Direct US Manufacturing Jobs Generated by Exports to United Arab Emirates (By Industry) 69
Appendix - Direct US Manufacturing Jobs Generated by Exports to United Arab Emirates (By Origin of Movement) 70
Appendix - Direct and Indirect US Jobs Generated by Manufactures Exports to United Arab Emirates (By Origin of Movement) 72
Appendix - Direct US Manufacturing Jobs Generated by Exports to the Saudi Arabian Market (By Industry) 74
Appendix - Direct US Manufacturing Jobs Generated by Exports to the Saudi Arabian Market (By Origin of Movement) 75
Appendix - Direct and Indirect US Jobs Generated by Manufactures Exports to Saudi Arabia (By Origin of Movement) ..77
Appendix - Direct US Manufacturing Jobs Generated by Exports to Egypt (By Industry) 79
Appendix - Direct US Manufacturing Jobs Generated by Exports to Egypt (By Origin of Movement) 80
Appendix - Direct and Indirect US Jobs Generated by Manufactures Exports to Egypt (By Origin of Movement) 82
Appendix - Direct US Manufacturing Jobs Generated by Exports to Kuwait (By Industry) 84
Appendix - Direct US Manufacturing Jobs Generated by Exports to Kuwait (By Origin of Movement) 85
Appendix - Direct and Indirect US Jobs Generated by Manufactures Exports to Kuwait (By Origin of Movement) 87
Appendix - Direct US Manufacturing Jobs Generated by Exports to Iraq (By Industry) 89
Appendix - Direct US Manufacturing Jobs Generated by Exports to Iraq (By Origin of Movement) 90
Appendix - Direct and Indirect US Jobs Generated by Manufactures Exports to Iraq (By Origin of Movement) 92
Appendix - Direct US Manufacturing Jobs Generated by Exports to Algeria (By Industry) 94
Appendix - Direct US Manufacturing Jobs Generated by Exports to Algeria (By Origin of Movement) 95
Appendix - Direct and Indirect US Jobs Generated by Manufactures Exports to Algeria (By Origin of Movement) 97
Appendix - Direct US Manufacturing Jobs Generated by Exports to Qatar (By Industry) 99
Appendix - Direct US Manufacturing Jobs Generated by Exports to Qatar (By Origin of Movement) 100

Appendix - Direct and Indirect US Jobs Generated by Manufactures Exports to Qatar (By Origin of Movement) 102
Appendix - Direct US Manufacturing Jobs Generated by Exports to Jordan (By Industry) 104
Appendix - Direct US Manufacturing Jobs Generated by Exports to Jordan (By Origin of Movement) 105
Appendix - Direct and Indirect US Jobs Generated by Manufactures Exports to Jordan (By Origin of Movement)...........107
Appendix - Direct US Manufacturing Jobs Generated by Exports to Oman (By Industry) 109
Appendix - Direct US Jobs Generated by Manufactures Exports to Oman (By Origin of Movement)...............................110
Appendix - Direct and Indirect US Jobs Generated by Manufactures Exports to Oman (By Origin of Movement) 112
Appendix - Direct US Manufacturing Jobs Generated by Exports to Morocco (By Industry) 114
Appendix - Direct US Manufacturing Jobs Generated by Exports to Morocco (By Origin of Movement) 115
Appendix - Direct and Indirect US Jobs Generated by Manufactures Exports to Morocco (By Origin of Movement).......117
Appendix - Direct US Manufacturing Jobs Generated by Exports to Lebanon (By Industry)....................................119
Appendix - Direct US Manufacturing Jobs Generated by Exports to Lebanon (By Origin of Movement)..........................120
Appendix - Direct and Indirect US Jobs Generated by Manufactures Exports to Lebanon (By Origin of Movement) 122
Appendix - Direct US Manufacturing Jobs Generated by Exports to Bahrain (By Industry) 124
Appendix - Direct US Manufacturing Jobs Generated by Exports to Bahrain (By Origin of Movement) 125
Appendix - Direct and Indirect US Jobs Generated by Manufactures Exports to Bahrain (By Origin of Movement).........127
Appendix - Direct US Manufacturing Jobs Generated by Exports to Tunisia (By Industry) 129
Appendix - Direct US Jobs Generated by Manufactures Exports to Tunisia (By Origin of Movement)...........................130
Appendix - Direct and Indirect US Jobs Generated by Manufactures Exports to Tunisia (By Origin of Movement) 132
Appendix - Direct US Manufacturing Jobs Generated by Exports to Yemen (By Industry) 134
Appendix - Direct US Manufacturing Jobs Generated by Exports to Yemen (By Origin of Movement) 135
Appendix - Direct and Indirect US Jobs Generated by Manufactures Exports to Yemen (By Origin of Movement)...........137
Appendix - Direct US Manufacturing Jobs Generated by Exports to Syria (By Industry) 139
Appendix - Direct US Manufacturing Jobs Generated by Exports to Syria (By Origin of Movement) 140
Appendix - Direct and Indirect US Jobs Generated by Manufactures Exports to Syria (By Origin of Movement)............142
Appendix - Direct US Manufacturing Jobs Generated by Exports to Sudan (By Industry).....................................144
Appendix - Direct US Manufacturing Jobs Generated by Exports to Sudan (By Origin of Movement)............................145
Appendix - Direct and Indirect US Jobs Generated by Manufactures Exports to Sudan (By Origin of Movement) 147
Appendix - Direct US Manufacturing Jobs Generated by Exports to Mauritania (By Industry) 149
Appendix - Direct US Manufacturing Jobs Generated by Exports to Mauritania (By Origin of Movement) 150
Appendix - Direct and Indirect US Jobs Generated by Manufactures Exports to Mauritania (By Origin of Movement)....152
Appendix - Direct US Manufacturing Jobs Generated by Exports to Libya (By Industry) 154
Appendix - Direct US Manufacturing Jobs Generated by Exports to Libya (By Origin of Movement)............................155
Appendix - Direct and Indirect US Jobs Generated by Manufactures Exports to Libya (By Origin of Movement)...........157
Appendix - Direct US Manufacturing Jobs Generated by Exports to Djibouti (By Industry) 159
Appendix - Direct US Manufacturing Jobs Generated by Exports to Djibouti (By Origin of Movement) 160
Appendix - Direct and Indirect US Jobs Generated by Manufactures Exports to Djibouti (By Origin of Movement).........162
Appendix - Direct US Manufacturing Jobs Generated by Exports to Somalia (By Industry)....................................164
Appendix - Direct US Manufacturing Jobs Generated by Exports to Somalia (By Origin of Movement).........................165
Appendix - Direct and Indirect US Jobs Generated by Manufactures Exports to Somalia (By Origin of Movement) 167
Appendix - Direct US Manufacturing Jobs Generated by Exports to Comoros (By Industry) 169
Appendix - Direct US Manufacturing Jobs Generated by Exports to Comoros (By Origin of Movement) 170
Appendix - Direct and Indirect US Jobs Generated by Manufactures Exports to Comoros (By Origin of Movement) 172
Appendix: Status Update: WTO and Bilateral U.S.-Arab Free Trade Agreements 179
Appendix: Saudi Executive Interviews - Nabeel Al Mojil..185
Appendix: Saudi Executive Interviews - Mohammed al-Misehal 187

Table of Figures

World Non-Immigrant Admissions into the United States...9
Arab Non-Immigrant Admissions into the United States...10
Non-Immigrant Visa Application: Hijacker Abdulaziz Alomari...12
Non-Immigrant Visa Appointment Wait Times (Working Days) 14
Non-Immigrant B-1 and B-2 Visa Processing (Working Days)..15
Non-Immigrant B-1 and B-2 Visa Benchmark Appointment and Processing Durations* 16
Non-Immigrant B-1 and B-2 Visa Validity Periods..16
Non-Immigrant B-1 and B-2 Visa Processing and Issuance Fees 16
Total Arab Market Merchandise Import Demand ($ US Billion)...19
Arab Business Traveler Admissions to the United States..20
Actual US Merchandise Exports to Arab Market, Best-Case Scenario, Opportunity Cost ($ US Billion)....21
US Direct Manufacturing Jobs from Arab Imports by Industry..22
Direct and Indirect Manufacturing-Related Jobs Created by US-Arab Trade 23
Arab Tourist Admissions to the United States 25
2005 Average International Visitor Length of Stay and Receipts 26
Estimated US Revenues Generated by Arab Tourist and Business Travelers and Opportunity Cost ($ US
    Million) 26
Estimated 2005 US Travel-Related Service Job Loss ($ US Million)...27
Arab Student Admissions into the United States...29
2005 Arab Student (F-1) Admissions into the United States 30
Arab Student F-1 (Education) Visa Validity Periods..31
Arab Student Enrollment in US Higher Education by Academic Year..31
Estimated US Revenues Generated by Arab Students, Best Case Scenario, Opportunity Cost ($ US Million)
   32
Fulbright Grants to Foreign Nationals...34
Actual US Merchandise Exports to UAE, Best Case Scenario, Opportunity Cost ($ US Billion) 38
US Merchandise Manufactures Exports to UAE by Industry Job Creation 41
Direct and Indirect Manufacturing Jobs Generated by Saudi Arabia in the US 45
US Merchandise Exports to Saudi Arabia, Best Case Scenario, Opportunity Cost ($ US Billion)................48
US Merchandise Manufactures Exports to Saudi Arabia by Industry Job Creation 48
Actual US Merchandise Exports to Egypt, Best Case Scenario, Opportunity Cost ($ US Billion) 50
Egypt Non-Immigrant Visa Processing Durations..51
Actual US Merchandise Exports to Kuwait, Best Case Scenario, Opportunity Cost ($ US Billion)..............52
Actual US Merchandise Exports to Algeria, Best Case Scenario, Opportunity Cost ($ US Billion) 53
Actual US Merchandise Exports to Qatar, Best Case Scenario, Opportunity Cost ($ US Billion).................54
Actual US Merchandise Exports to Iraq, Best Case Scenario, Opportunity Cost ($ US Billion) 56
Current Status of Arab Market WTO Membership, BITs, TIFAs and FTAs...180
U.S. Merchandise Exports to Jordan –Five Years Before and After 2000 FTA..182

Recommendations

RECOMMENDATION #1: NATIONAL SECURITY MUST BE THE FIRST AND MOST IMPORTANT CRITERION IN REVIEWING NON-IMMIGRANT VISA APPLICATIONS. NO OUTSOURCING OR PROCESS IMPROVEMENTS SHOULD COMPROMISE US NATIONAL SECURITY. HOWEVER, ADEQUATE INVESTMENTS IN THE SECURITY REVIEW PROCESS MUST BE MADE TO ELIMINATE THIS CORE RESOURCE SHORTAGE BOTTLENECK THAT IS CAUSING INCREASED PROCESS DURATIONS. 13

RECOMMENDATION #2: CONSULAR HUMAN RESOURCES (1 EMPLOYEE FOR EVERY 4,000 SUCCESSFUL APPLICANTS) ARE CURRENTLY INSUFFICIENT TO EFFICIENTLY PROCESS ARAB MARKET VISAS IN A TIMELY, PROFESSIONAL MANNER. THE US CONGRESS SHOULD STUDY THE MASSIVE OPPORTUNITY COSTS OF LENGTHY PROCESSING DELAYS ON THE US ECONOMY AND INCREASE BUDGETS IN ORDER TO PROPERLY STAFF AND PROCESS VISAS. 17

RECOMMENDATION #3: A PROACTIVE VISA PROMOTION PROGRAM SHOULD BE CREATED TO PLACE NEW "E-3" VISAS IN THE HANDS OF INDIVIDUALS WHO HAVE A STRONG INFLUENCE ON US-ARAB TRADE: KEY EXECUTIVES, BUSINESS LEADERS, GOVERNMENT LEADERS, AND EDUCATORS IN THE ARAB MARKET. THIS PROACTIVE EXTENSION OF US VISAS TO PEOPLE WHOM THE US MOST WANTS TO SEE DOING BUSINESS AND INTERCULTURAL EXCHANGE WOULD CHANGE THE PARADIGM OF VISA PROCESSING FROM A "PULL" SYSTEM IN WHICH WEARY EXECUTIVES NAVIGATE AN UNPLEASANT BUREAUCRACY OF US CONSULAR SERVICES TO A BUSINESS-ORIENTED "PUSH" SYSTEM IN WHICH US COMPETITIVENESS AND MARKET PROMOTION IS UNLEASHED INTO THE VISA PROCESS. US CORPORATIONS AND UNIVERSITIES SHOULD BE ASKED TO RECOMMEND INDIVIDUALS WHO SHOULD BE OFFERED PERMANENT E-3 VISAS. 17

RECOMMENDATION #4: GIVEN THE IMPORTANCE OF NON-IMMIGRANT VISAS TO THE US ECONOMY, A "VISA PROCESS REVIEW BOARD" COMPOSED OF CORPORATIONS, UNIVERSITY ADMINISTRATORS, TRADE AND INDUSTRY ASSOCIATIONS, AND OTHER OUTSIDE EXPERTS SHOULD BE CONVENED TO REVIEW CONSULAR NON-IMMIGRANT VISA PROCESS EFFICIENCY AND PROPOSE IMPROVEMENTS. 20

RECOMMENDATION #5: CONGRESSIONAL REPRESENTATIVES FROM THE FOURTEEN KEY STATES NEED TO BECOME MORE ACTIVE IN VISA PROCESS OVERSIGHT ON BEHALF OF STATE INDUSTRIES AND FAMILIES DEPENDENT ON US-ARAB TRADE. A NEW "US-ARAB TRADE AND ECONOMIC PROSPERITY" CAUCUS MADE UP OF PRO-DEVELOPMENT CONGRESSIONAL REPRESENTATIVES SHOULD BE FORMED TO MONITOR AND REMOVE VISA AND OTHER NON-TARIFF TRADE BARRIERS. 23

RECOMMENDATION #6: THE US MUST REVERSE ARAB STUDENT DECLINES THROUGH A TWO-PART STRATEGY. IT MUST APPLY SUFFICIENT ADDITIONAL VISA PROCESSING RESOURCES TO ACCELERATE THE ADMISSION OF QUALIFIED, CREDENTIALED STUDENTS FROM THE REGION AND REDUCE APPLICANT BACKLOGS. THE US MUST ALSO BRING IN LARGER NUMBERS OF ARAB STUDENTS THROUGH DIVERSIFIED SCHOLARSHIP GRANT DISTRIBUTION. GRANTS SHOULD SEEK TO INCREASE THE NUMBER OF STUDENTS FROM COUNTRIES THAT HAVE HISTORICALLY SENT FEW STUDENTS TO THE US. 33

RECOMMENDATION #7: THE US STATE DEPARTMENT AND FULBRIGHT FOREIGN SCHOLARSHIP BOARD SHOULD DOUBLE THE NUMBER OF ARAB SCHOLARSHIP GRANTS AND REPRIORITIZE THEIR DISTRIBUTION TOWARD COUNTRIES WHOSE TRADE POTENTIAL AND REGIONAL INFLUENCE HAS NOT HISTORICALLY BEEN REFLECTED IN FULBRIGHT ALLOTMENTS. GRANT DISTRIBUTION CRITERIA SHOULD AIM TO ATTRACT WORTHY SCHOLARS FROM HISTORICALLY UNDERREPRESENTED COUNTRIES LIKE THE UAE AND LIBYA WHERE NO FOREIGN STUDENT RECOVERY PROGRAM (LIKE SAUDI ARABIA'S) CURRENTLY EXISTS. 35

RECOMMENDATION #8: CURRENTLY, THE EVAF IS CUTTING DATA ENTRY OVERHEAD IN THE CONSULATE, BUT DOES NOT DELIVER ADDED TIME SAVINGS FOR VISA APPLICANTS. THE EVAF NEEDS TO ARRIVE AT A DEVELOPMENT STAGE IN WHICH SUCCESSFUL DATA TRANSMISSION INITIATES BACK-OFFICE VISA PROCESSING, PARTICULARLY SECURITY REVIEWS, AND CUTS OVERALL APPLICATION PROCESSING TIME. 38

RECOMMENDATION #9: THE FAILED DPW ACQUISITION REVEALS THAT INTERESTED PARTIES CAN SUCCESSFULLY ORCHESTRATE NEGATIVE CAMPAIGNS BASED ON FALSE "NATIONAL SECURITY" ISSUES RAISED BY DOMESTIC COMPETITORS. THIS RAISES THE POSSIBILITY OF SIMILAR FALSE ALARMS RAISED BY FOREIGN INTELLIGENCE SERVICES. CIA AND FBI SECURITY VISA APPLICATION SECURITY REVIEWS THAT DRAW UPON FOREIGN SOURCE INTELLIGENCE SHOULD NOT RELY ON SOURCES THAT ARE ARAB MARKET RIVALS OR COMPETITORS: BAD INTELLIGENCE LEADS TO VISA REJECTION AND DRIVES A WEDGE BETWEEN THE US AND KEY ARAB BUSINESS LEADERS. 44

About the Author

Grant F. Smith is director of research at the Institute for Research: Middle Eastern Policy (IRmep). IRmep is a Washington D.C.-based nonprofit organization established in 2002 that analyzes the US foreign policy formulation process. Smith's research, analysis and forecasts of trade, market size, opportunity cost, and international business strategy have appeared in the Financial Times of London, Reuters, Inc. Magazine, Arab News, Gannet, The Wall Street Journal, the New York Times, the Daily Star, the Associated Press, and specialty publications such as the US State Department's "Washington File." Smith has personally appeared on Voice of America (VOA) television, C-SPAN, and CNN as well as public radio programs.

Smith's research has taken him to more than forty countries, on assignments ranging from as little as a few days to a half-decade. Before joining IRmep, he was a senior analyst and later a program manager and consultant at the Boston-based Yankee Group Research, Inc., where he worked on investments of over $3 billion in development projects in thirty countries in conjunction with private corporations, investment banks, and NGOs.

Before that, he worked as a marketing manager at the Minneapolis-based Investors Diversified Services (IDS), now Ameriprise Financial Advisors. Smith's formal education includes a BA in International Relations from the University of Minnesota and a master's degree in International Management from the University of St. Thomas in St Paul, Minnesota. Smith's career in research includes the authorship of over 140 research papers, articles, and editorials on international issues.

1.0 Executive Summary

Visa processing barriers limiting inbound international business and pleasure travelers cost the United States economy billions of dollars in direct revenues while severing vital communications links to the Arab market. The Institute for Research: Middle Eastern Policy (IRmep) has gathered the most authoritative current data and statistics about visitor flows from twenty-two Arab League countries to the US before and after 9/11. We present quantitative findings on the economic impact of increasing visa trade barriers in terms of actual versus potential US exports to the region, diverted travel industry revenues, fewer foreign students in the higher education system, and lost US manufacturing jobs.

- **Total Arab market import demand has more than doubled since the year 2001, but US corporations attempting to close deals are stymied by visa barriers that turn away even longtime Arab business visitors, including trainees seeking to enter the US. The US has already lost US$62 billion in merchandise trade to competitors maintaining "open door" visa policies through 2005.**
- **Cumulative opportunity cost losses are on track to reach a total of $101 billion in 2006 as "turnkey" infrastructure projects, defense, consumer goods, and industrial machinery deals flow to US competitors. For some key energy producing countries such as Saudi Arabia, every visitor wrongly denied a US visa costs an average of $1.4 million in lost merchandise trade.**
- **Arab nonimmigrant entry into the US for business and pleasure is only half (52%) of year 2001 levels, creating direct five-year travel-related service losses of US$1.775 billion to the US economy and eliminating 4,126 potential travel related service jobs.**
- **In 2005, Arab student enrollments in the US higher education system reached only 66% of their 2001 level. The US higher education system has lost $1.989 billion in revenue and just fewer than 9,000 education and support services jobs. More importantly, the pipeline of future business and government leaders in the region is no longer oriented toward the US system, goods or services.**
- **The direct and indirect effects of lost manufacturing jobs materially impact the economic health of states across the nation. In 2005, UAE imports from the US sustained 63,619 jobs, while Saudi Arabia's merchandise imports sustained 60,269 direct manufacturing jobs and indirect upstream and downstream jobs.**
- **Total US direct and indirect jobs supported by manufactured goods exports to the Arab market were 215,000 in 2005, but could have reached 420,000 with more effective US visa policies.**

United States visa processing in the Arab world, formerly driven by security outsourcing and lack of due diligence, has now become both unresponsive and overly restrictive in many key markets. IRmep recommends avoiding permanent damage to vital trade and communications links between the US and the Arab market by adequately resourcing visa processing for potential visitors from this key region.

2.0 Free Travel and Free Trade: The US National Interest

Executives and pleasure travelers have two choices in a post-9/11 world: they can let fear of terror attacks dampen their desire to travel internationally in search of business and recreational opportunities, or they can overcome irrational fears while being conscious that the world has changed.

Governments also have two major choices regarding international travel: they can shut down or slow visitor flow, citing process blockage by national security concerns, or they can facilitate international travel under secure visa processing.

Business and tourism trends reveal that after a slight two-year slump, world travelers are eager to seek cultural and commercial enrichment through international travel, particularly to the United States. In 2005, non-immigrant (temporary) business and pleasure traveler admissions into the US reached 32.0 million, slightly less than the 32.8 million entries during the year 2001.

World Non-Immigrant Admissions into the United States

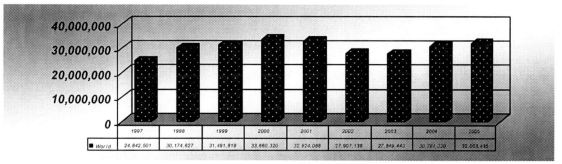

	1997	1998	1999	2000	2001	2002	2003	2004	2005
World	24,842,501	30,174,627	31,491,819	33,660,320	32,824,088	27,907,139	27,849,443	30,781,330	32,553,435

(Source: Yearbook of Immigration Statistics, Department of Homeland Security)
However, one region of the world remains largely shut out of the US. Executives and tourists originating in Arab countries must run an opaque gauntlet of barriers to acquire or renew their US entry visas. Arab non-immigrant entries, which peaked at 314,786 in the year 2001, are nowhere near recovery. In 2005, non-immigrant entries from the 22-country Arab League reached only 176,416.

Arab Non-Immigrant Admissions into the United States
(Source: Yearbook of Immigration Statistics, Department of Homeland Security)

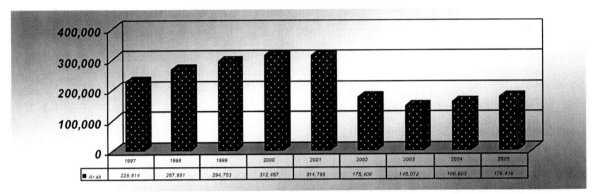

Year	1997	1998	1999	2000	2001	2002	2003	2004	2005
Arab	228,814	267,881	294,753	312,467	314,786	175,409	146,072	166,603	176,416

Denial of non-immigrant visas to travelers has become one of the most significant non-tariff trade barriers between the US and Arab market. Visas can become a trade barrier, since trade barriers include any government policy or regulation that restricts international trade. Traditional trade barriers include import duties, import licenses, export licenses, quotas, tariffs, and subsidies. However, as WTO membership and free trade agreements have increased other non-tariff barriers can emerge as the dominant roadblocks to trade and economic development.

US visa restrictions are emerging as the major non-tariff barrier and can be even more restrictive than traditional tariff barriers. Most trade tariff barriers work on the same principle: the imposition of some sort of cost on trade that raises the price of the traded products. Restrictions on visitor flow can be even more severe. If regional automobile distributors cannot travel to Michigan and other key manufacturing states to strategize over new model launches and service strategies, the distribution network begins to falter and crumble. Engineer and plant owner access to major industrial machinery manufacturers in the US is also vital to the purchase process. Cutting this link of repeat visits for research and vendor selection shuts the US out of a booming market.

Over the long term, the US visa trade barrier could lead to a more traditional trade war as Arab states impose their own restrictions on US travelers or seek to retaliate on key exports with traditional tariff-oriented restrictions of their own. Looming trade barriers could jeopardize President George W. Bush's vision of a free trade area covering the entire Middle East by 2013. Currently, the US has signed bilateral free trade agreements with Bahrain, Jordan, Morocco, and Oman. Serious negotiations are underway with Egypt, Kuwait, Qatar, and UAE. Under the Bush vision, the FTA building blocks would ultimately create a united Middle East Free Trade Area (MEFTA).

Trade barriers of any kind decrease overall economic efficiency. In a competitive global market, countries erecting trade barriers are ultimately unable to leverage their comparative advantages. While it can be legitimate to raise a barrier in the case of quantifiable health or national security threats, a careful look at visa delays and denials reveals why the barrier is growing: inadequate security review resources. In the absence of accurate opportunity cost data, some US policymakers may believe that cutting visitor flow from the Arab market by half or more through inadequate security review resources is reasonable. However, when the true post-9/11 opportunity costs are revealed, they are clearly too high.

Non-immigrant visa processing in the Arab market was once defined by incompetence and outsourcing. An in-depth review of the non-immigrant visa application of 9/11 hijacker Abdouliziz Alomari reveals that the application was not only incomplete, but contained five red flags that should have led to rejection. If the US State Department officials based in Saudi Arabia had followed processes and laws on the books for reviewing non-immigrant visa applications, at least 15 of the 19 hijackers Al-Qaeda recruited from Saudi Arabia would have been denied visas. This means that a critical mass of Al-Qaeda recruits wouldn't have been able to enter the United States to carry out the attacks on September 11, 2001, according to a thorough review of DS-156 applications conducted by four former US consular officials.[1]

In 2001, the US State Department not only failed to maintain minimal levels of quality management over the visa application process, it was actively attempting to outsource most of the process (including critical face-to-face interviews) to travel agencies through its new "Visa Express" program.[2] US Embassy officials in Saudi Arabia began the Visa Express program in June 2001 to reduce long lines of applicants while relieving consular officials of clerical overhead. Visa Express relied on 10 designated travel agencies to review all applications for accuracy and completeness. Travel agencies then forwarded the passports, applications, and fees to the US consulate; most visas were issued within twenty hours with no face-to-face interview. Three of the 9/11 hijackers entered the U.S. through the security holes opened by the Visa Express program and were never personally interviewed by a US consular officer.

---

1 Visas that Should Have Been Denied http://www.nationalreview.com/mowbray/mowbray100902.asp

2 Homeland Security Department to Oversee Visa Program, http://www.washingtonpost.com/wp-dyn/articles/A47861-2002Aug5.html

Non-Immigrant Visa Application: Hijacker Abdulaziz Alomari

(Sources: US State Department, and the National Review)

Red Flag #1 Refusing to answer nationality or even gender should have led to automatic visa rejection.

Red Flag #2 Applicant's address (a hotel) reveals he is a transient who should be assumed to be an immigrant rather than non-immigrant

Red Flag #3 Applicant indicates he is married but does not complete required "name of spouse" field.

Red Flag #4 Applicant claims he is a "student" but leaves field for school "name and street address" blank.

Red Flag #5 Applicant claims self as the source of financial support, but provides no documention of financial assets for the trip.

No consular officer comments.

The US consulate in Saudi Arabia showed a monumental lack of due diligence in granting visas to the 9/11 hijackers. However, incompetence in visa reviews has now been replaced by near-paralysis as the Department of Homeland Security's new processes and delays keep legitimate travelers, such as engineers, executives, and students, out of the US and in a state of limbo. Over the long term, this new barrier will break longstanding US ties to regional leaders, thinkers, and businesspeople, who will become less knowledgeable and less attracted to the "American way." Placing visa applicants in limbo can only be seen as a victory for the terrorists who purposely recruited Saudi hijackers in an attempt to create a schism between the US and an important cultural, religious and energy development center in the Arab world. The negative economic and cultural impact brought on by the attacks is now evident across manufacturing, travel-related service, and education sectors in the US.

According to the State Department, there are 215 visa issuance centers around the world with 8,000 employees. *Thirty-two million non-immigrants visited the US in the year 2005—4,000 for every front-line US visa official.*[3]

The same pressures, bottlenecks, and delays that led US officials to undercut national security in favor of outsourcing in the year 2001 have returned. Arab visitors typically plan for travel well in advance, but waiting times for interview appointments, a vital step in acquiring a visa, have increased. Non-immigrant visa wait times have reached 49 working days—almost 2.5 months—in Saudi Arabia. Egyptians, who represented 21% of Arab non-immigrant entries to the US in 2001, wait a month on average to secure an appointment.

The solution to long waiting times and lost economic opportunities does not require cutting corners on security. Rather, the economic cost benefit ratio of visits by foreign non-immigrants should be clearly understood, and the proper amount of resources should then be brought to bear to securely process each visa. In the case of Saudi Arabia, the opportunity cost is now clear: in 2005, every wrongly denied visa cost the US $1.4 million on average. Currently, the US does not invest enough resources in the visa security review process to minimize subjectivity, uncertainty, and unwarranted rejections.

Recommendation #1: National security must be the first and most important criterion in reviewing non-immigrant visa applications. No outsourcing or process improvements should compromise US national security. However, adequate investments in the security review process must be made to eliminate this core resource shortage bottleneck that is causing increased process durations.

---

3 The Arab American News. Dearborn, Mich.: Dec 3-Dec 9, 2005. Vol. 21, Iss. 1034; pg. 15

Non-Immigrant Visa Appointment Wait Times (Working Days)[4]

(Source: US State Department, August 2006)

Country	Non-Immigrant Visa Appointment	Student Visa Appointment	Other Appointment
Saudi Arabia	49	98	49
Yemen	45	5	5
Egypt	18	1	18
Morocco	15	0	15
Jordan	11	11	11
Qatar	7	0	0
Djibouti	5	2	5
Kuwait	4	3	4
UAE	2	0	2
Algeria	1	1	1
Syria	1	1	1
Bahrain	0	0	0
Oman	0	0	0
Tunisia	0	0	0
Mauritania	0	0	0

Obtaining and successfully completing an interview does not guarantee applicants a visa, even for longtime repeat visitors to the US. Applicants must wait another 31-37 working days after interviews for regular processing and possible "special clearance" scrutiny before the US consular division decides whether to grant a visa. According to Martin Tatuch of the US State Department's Visa Office, approximately 2.5% of all applicants are deemed suspicious enough to warrant special clearance.[5] People can be flagged for special clearance if their names appear in a very large database maintained by the US State Department or if their responses trigger certain screens that require further investigation. Special clearances typically require FBI and CIA screening. 98% of special clearances are completed within a month.

There is a further possibility that applicants will not be denied a visa, but will not be granted a visa. A number of screens used by the government are temporary in nature, creating a growing informal category of applicants who wait for years with no clear timeline or pathway toward a visa. This limbo pool is particularly acute and growing in Saudi Arabia (see page 39).

---

4 Does not include processing time

5 The Arab American News. Dearborn, Mich.: Dec 3-Dec 9, 2005. Vol. 21, Iss. 1034; pg. 15

Non-Immigrant B-1 and B-2 Visa Processing (Working Days)[6]
(Source: US State Department, August 2006)

Country	Visa Processing	Special Clearance	Total Potential
Saudi Arabia	7	30	37
Jordan	2	30	32
Kuwait	1	30	31
Eqypt	2	30	32
Morocco	1	30	31
UAE	1	30	31
Bahrain	1	30	31
Tunisia	1	30	31
Oman	2	30	32
Syria	1	30	31
Qatar	2	30	32
Yemen	4	30	34
Algeria	1	30	31

If a person's name is similar to that of a suspected terrorist or international crime figure, his or her visa can be denied or the application can be thrown into limbo. Process timelines for name checks vary. For immigrant visas, the FBI name check process can last for months or years, depending on the individual.[7] Visa seekers have no recourse to clear their names, since no specific reason for refusal is usually given, a step that protects the sources and methods of the background check process.

The main reason for most rejections is that the non-immigrant applicant did not sufficiently establish his or her intention to return to the country of origin. Non-immigrant applicants are essentially "guilty until proven innocent" under the current system. According to Section 214 (b) of the US Code:

> "...every alien shall be presumed to be an immigrant until he establishes to the satisfaction of the consular officer, at the time of application for admission, that he is entitled to a nonimmigrant status."

Finally, simply holding a non-immigrant visa does not guarantee ingress at any port of entry. Non-immigrant visa holders may be denied entry if officials at US ports of entry decide it is in the interest of US national security.

---

6 US consulates in Beirut and Baghdad were not offering visa processing services at the time this report was written.

7 Kuwait evacuee stymied in U.S. citizenship bid   http://www.telegram.com/apps/pbcs.dll/article?AID=/20060906/NEWS/609060660/1116

Non-Immigrant B-1 and B-2 Visa Benchmark Appointment and Processing Durations*

(Source: US State Department, August 2006)

Country	Visa Processing Duration (Days)
Saudi Arabia	74
Egypt, Syria, Yemen	64
Kuwait, UAE, Bahrain, Tunisia, Oman, Qatar	62
Morocco, Algeria	60

Potential visitors who are granted visas may find their flexibility regarding travel dates or ability to return to the United States vastly restricted in the post-9/11 world. Five-year multiple-entry visas, once the norm, are now routinely granted only to entrants from Tunisia, Morocco, UAE, Qatar, and Kuwait. Many key US regional trading partners are granted visas valid for only 12-60 months, adding to the queue of repeat applicants and contributing to the problem of long appointment lead times and processing periods.

Non-Immigrant B-1 and B-2 Visa Validity Periods

(Source: US State Department, August 2006)

Country	Visa Validity Period (Months)
Tunisia, Morocco, UAE, Qatar	120
Mauritania, Bahrain, Jordan, Egypt, Lebanon	60
Saudi Arabia, Oman, Syria	24
Djibouti, Yemen	12
Iraq, Libya, Somolia, Algeria, Sudan	3
Comoros	2

The United States charges a standard fee of $100 for processing B-1 (business) and B-2 (pleasure) visas. Additional fees may be charged on a reciprocal basis: because countries such as Sudan and Yemen charge additional issuing fees for visas requested by US citizens, the United States charges similar fees to citizens of these countries.

Non-Immigrant B-1 and B-2 Visa Processing and Issuance Fees

(Source: US State Department, August 2006)

Country	Reciprocal Issuance Fee (US)
Sudan	$50
Comoros	$31
Yemen	$30
Oman	$15
Libya	$10
Saudi Arabia	$7

The US offers a "Visa Waiver" program to citizens of a number of key trading partner countries (most located in Europe) that have a long-term non-immigrant rejection rate of less than 3%[8]. Visa Waiver status is granted when US law enforcement concerns, low visa application rejection rates, and commercial concerns warrant.

Recommendation #2: Consular human resources (1 employee for every 4,000 successful applicants) are currently insufficient to efficiently process Arab market visas in a timely, professional manner. The US Congress should study the massive opportunity costs of lengthy processing delays on the US economy and increase budgets in order to properly staff and process visas.

The US and most other developed countries offer a broad range of non-immigrant visa categories, some of which recognize the value of individuals who positively impact trade and investment (see Non-Immigrant Visa Categories in the Appendix). The Immigration and Nationality Act extends non-immigrant visa status for a national who is coming to the United States to carry on substantial trade (E-1 Treaty Trader visa), including trade in services or technology, principally between the United States and another country. The E-2 Treaty Trader visa is extended to individuals who develop and direct the operations of an enterprise in which the national has invested or are in the process of investing a substantial amount of capital.[9]

Given the high average economic impact of Arab market visitors to the US, the US should proactively facilitate greater numbers of E-1 and E-2 visas based on estimated future trade impact and create a special third class of visa.

Recommendation #3: A proactive visa promotion program should be created to place new "E-3" visas in the hands of individuals who have a strong influence on US-Arab trade: key executives, business leaders, government leaders, and educators in the Arab market. This proactive extension of US visas to people whom the US most wants to see doing business and intercultural exchange would change the paradigm of visa processing from a "pull" system in which weary executives navigate an unpleasant bureaucracy of US consular services to a business-oriented "push" system in which US competitiveness and market promotion is unleashed into the visa process. US corporations and universities

---

8 U.S. visa policy is a passport to reduced competitiveness, Chicago Sun – Times, September 20, 2006. p. 43

9 US State Department Treaty Traders, http://travel.state.gov/visa/temp/types/types_1273.html

should be asked to recommend individuals who should be offered permanent E-3 visas.

Finally, as a family oriented culture that typically travels in groups, it should be understood that splitting families by granting some members a non-immigrant visa and not others, is the equivalent of granting no visa.

"The process has a dramatic negative change after 9/11. When visa processing takes less than 24 hours to be processed (at the US consulate in Dhahran) before 9/11, takes now more than 2 to 3 weeks in normal cases, and 2 to 3 months in other cases (In Riyadh Embassy)! Then yes, there is a change! Provided that when a family applies for a tourism visa before 9/11, they'll never be surprised by rejecting a child and his mom, and at the same time for the same application, accepting a teen age boy and his father of the same family for the entry visa! I see this as an inconsistent mess. With my respect of course!" **Mohammed al-Misehal, VP of Al-Misehal Telecommunications, Riyadh**

3.0 The Trade Consequences of US Visa Barriers

As visa interview waiting times, processing durations, and rejection rates are increasing, the Arab market demand for imports has taken off and is expected to more than double in the period from 2001 to 2006. Arab market purchasing power, buoyed by higher energy prices on the world market, has led to explosive regional demand for infrastructure, industrial machinery, and sophisticated consumer goods.

Total Arab Market Merchandise Import Demand ($ US Billion)
(Sources: CIA World Factbook, National Accounts, World Bank, and Institute for Research: Middle Eastern Policy, Inc.)

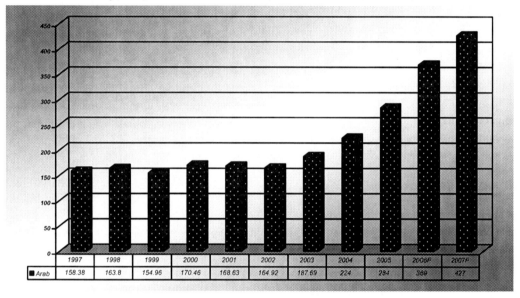

	1997	1998	1999	2000	2001	2002	2003	2004	2005	2006F	2007F
Arab	158.38	163.8	154.96	170.46	168.63	164.92	187.69	224	284	369	427

Arab demand weakened slightly in 2002, only to spring back in 2003. However, as demand has increased, the climate between the US and the Arab market has become more negative. US policymakers have tightened visa screening criteria while severely limiting the human and background check resources available in key trading partner states. This has led to longer waiting periods even while competitor markets in Asia and Western Europe have maintained an "open-door" policy for Arab buyers.

Recommendation #4: Given the importance of non-immigrant visas to the US economy, a "Visa Process Review Board" composed of corporations, university administrators, trade and industry associations, and other outside experts should be convened to review consular non-immigrant visa process efficiency and propose improvements.

Arab Business Traveler Admissions to the United States
(Source: Yearbook of Immigration Statistics, Department of Homeland Security)

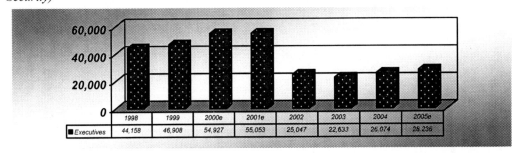

	1998	1999	2000e	2001e	2002	2003	2004	2005e
■ Executives	44,158	46,908	54,927	55,053	25,047	22,633	26,074	28,235

Entry into the US market by Arab wholesale buyers, project engineers, educators, and regional development leaders has been stymied by delays and rejections. Between 1998 and 2001, admission levels were spiraling upward for executives from the region visiting US suppliers, attending economic development conferences, and financing passive and direct investments. However, by the year 2005, Arab business traveler entries into the US had fallen to only half (51.3%) of 2001 levels.

The correlation between ease of Arab executive travel to the US and US merchandise exports to the Arab market is almost perfect: US merchandise exports to the region are at half the level they could have reached under a more effective US visa processing regime.

Even Arab executives who possess multiple-entry visas are no longer short listing US industrial machinery vendors. One well-known businessman heading a large publicly traded Saudi industrial conglomerate met with a US consultant visiting Saudi Arabia to review a tender for $250 million of equipment. The Saudi executive said the only tender restriction was "no American companies," since Saudi technicians might not be admitted to the United States for training. **The service component is an integral part of most industrial equipment deals. "No visas" increasingly means "no deal."[10]**

Tighter restrictions on Arab industrial buyers have directly impacted US merchandise exports, which have not kept pace with regional demand growth. The US share of the market, on a positive growth curve before 2001, has flattened. Total US exports to the region reached the pinnacle of an

---

10 http://www.saudi-us-relations.org/articles/2006/interviews/060712-qunaibet-interview.html

accelerated upswing in the year 2001 as Arab countries looked to US service providers, industrial manufacturers, and other makers of capital goods. By stemming the exchange of people, capital, and goods with the region, the US will miss a total of $101 billion in merchandise export opportunities through the year 2006 as regional demand for consumer and industrial goods surges past US providers. This is an economic impact equivalent to shutting down the <u>entire US tourism industry</u>. (As we'll see in the next section, the US already <u>has</u> shut down a significant portion of tourism flow from the Arab market.)[11]

Actual US Merchandise Exports to Arab Market, Best-Case Scenario, Opportunity Cost ($ US Billion)

(Sources: US Census International Trade Division, Institute for Research: Middle Eastern Policy, Inc.)

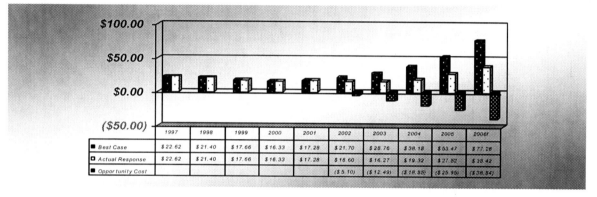

	1997	1998	1999	2000	2001	2002	2003	2004	2005	2006f
■ Best Case	$ 22.62	$ 21.40	$ 17.66	$ 16.33	$ 17.28	$ 21.70	$ 28.76	$ 38.18	$ 53.47	$ 77.26
□ Actual Response	$ 22.62	$ 21.40	$ 17.66	$ 16.33	$ 17.28	$ 16.60	$ 16.27	$ 19.32	$ 27.52	$ 38.42
■ Opportunity Cost						($ 5.10)	($ 12.49)	($ 18.85)	($ 25.95)	($ 38.84)

This missed opportunity would have created 419,865 direct and indirect manufacturing jobs in the US.

Among the hardest hit stakeholders are sophisticated manufacturing industries that provide high-wage jobs while generating abundant upstream and downstream economic activity, as well as industry diversification and taxes to the local economy.

Affected Industries

The US's beleaguered passenger automobile and truck industries currently depend on Arab market imports for almost 25,000 manufacturing jobs. 18,000 direct manufacturing jobs are supported by industrial machinery exports, while nearly 7,000 direct jobs are created in the computer and information technology industry.

---

11 Travel Industry Fun Facts http://www.tia.org/pressmedia/fun_facts.html

US Direct Manufacturing Jobs from Arab Imports by Industry
(Source: Institute for Research: Middle Eastern Policy, Inc.)

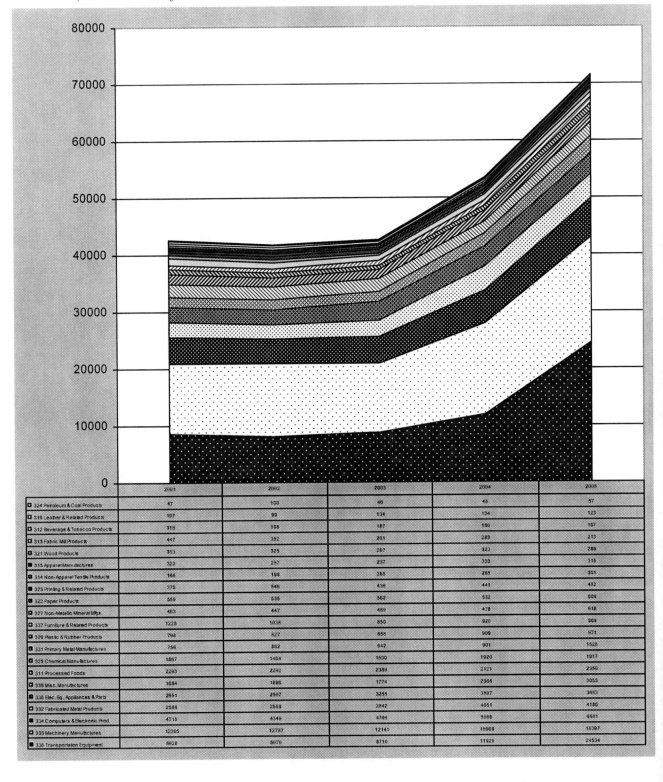

	2001	2002	2003	2004	2005
324 Petroleum & Coal Products	47	108	46	48	57
316 Leather & Related Products	107	99	134	134	123
312 Beverage & Tobacco Products	318	198	187	186	167
313 Fabric Mill Products	447	382	261	283	213
321 Wood Products	313	325	267	323	289
315 Apparel Manufactures	323	237	237	333	315
314 Non-Apparel Textile Products	168	199	265	265	351
323 Printing & Related Products	375	546	436	441	452
322 Paper Products	559	535	562	532	609
327 Non-Metallic Mineral Mfgs.	463	447	489	478	618
337 Furniture & Related Products	1225	1038	850	928	969
326 Plastic & Rubber Products	798	827	858	909	971
331 Primary Metal Manufactures	756	862	642	901	1528
325 Chemical Manufactures	1867	1464	1530	1920	1917
311 Processed Foods	2293	2292	2389	2121	2358
339 Misc. Manufactures	1684	1896	1774	2368	3053
335 Elec. Eq. Appliances & Parts	2681	2507	3255	3507	3683
332 Fabricated Metal Products	2588	2559	2842	4051	4186
334 Computers & Electronic Prod.	4715	4349	4766	5868	6681
333 Machinery Manufactures	12305	12787	12141	15969	16397
336 Transportation Equipment	8628	8078	8710	11929	24534

Key US State Stakeholders

A number of states are key beneficiaries of the direct and indirect manufacturing jobs created by US-Arab merchandise trade. In 2005, fourteen US states had more than 5,000 jobs supported by merchandise exports to the Arab market. The leading state, Texas, had 44,719 jobs dependent on US-Arab trade, followed by California (18,249) and New York (16,923).

Direct and Indirect Manufacturing-Related Jobs Created by US-Arab Trade
(Sources: May 2006 US Census Bureau Report, "Exports from Manufacturing Establishments" and Institute for Research: Middle Eastern Policy, Inc.)

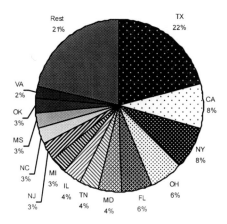

Recommendation #5: Congressional representatives from the fourteen key states need to become more active in visa process oversight on behalf of state industries and families dependent on US-Arab trade. A new "US-Arab Trade and Economic Prosperity" caucus made up of pro-development congressional representatives should be formed to monitor and remove visa and other non-tariff trade barriers.

4.0 Turning Away the World's Highest-Spending Tourists

Two vital US service sectors have also been hit hard by restrictive visa processes: tourism and higher education.

Arab Tourist Admissions to the United States
(Source: Yearbook of Immigration Statistics, Department of Homeland Security)

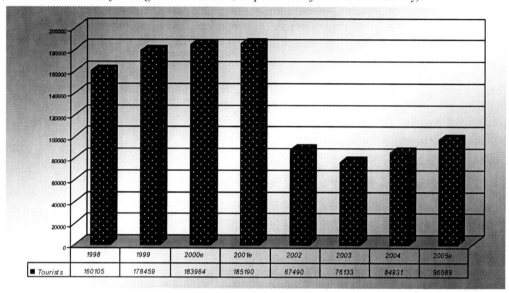

	1998	1999	2000e	2001e	2002	2003	2004	2005e
■ Tourists	160105	178459	183964	185190	87490	76133	84931	95589

International travelers spent $93 billion in the US in 2004, according to the Travel Industry Association (TIA). The travel and tourism industry is one of America's largest service exports and among the few industries generating a positive balance of trade for the US, reaching approximately $4 billion in 2004.

Within this tourism ecosystem, travelers originating from the Middle East have historically stayed longer and produced more receipts than visitors from any other region. **Each Saudi visitor spends an average of $9,368 per US visit.**[12] This is 300% more than any other nationality of visitor, according to the US Department of Commerce, and boosts the average spending level of Middle East visitors to the US above that of visitors from other regions tracked by the US Office of Travel and Tourism Industries.

---

12 "Arab travel to the U.S. declines" Wall Street Journal (Europe). Brussels: Apr 21, 2006. p. 8

2005 Average International Visitor Length of Stay and Receipts[13]
(Source: US Office of Travel and Tourism Industries)

	Length of Stay (Days)	Receipts per Visitor
Middle East	25.0	$3,206
Western Europe	14.7	$2,979
South America	20.2	$1,818
Asia (66% from Japan)	14.7	$1,661

Even with an inevitable global downturn in 2002, pro-tourism visa policies for this high-spending region would have added a billion dollars to US industry revenues by the year 2005. Instead, treating Arab visitors as suspects rather than prospects has driven tourists away from historically high-interest attractions such as Disneyland and Manhattan and toward other world vacation destinations. Between 2002 and 2005, restrictive tourist visa policies cost the US $1.8 billion in lost revenue.

Estimated US Revenues Generated by Arab Tourist and Business Travelers and Opportunity Cost ($ US Million)
(Sources: US Office of Travel and Tourism Industries, Department of Homeland Security and Institute for Research: Middle Eastern Policy, Inc.)

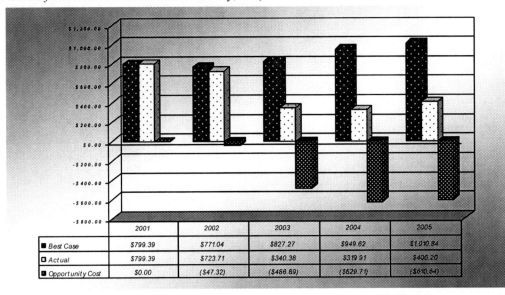

	2001	2002	2003	2004	2005
Best Case	$799.39	$771.04	$827.27	$949.62	$1,010.84
Actual	$799.39	$723.71	$340.38	$319.91	$400.20
Opportunity Cost	$0.00	($47.32)	($486.89)	($629.71)	($610.64)

Arab tourist and business travelers supported 2,729 travel-related service jobs in the US in the year 2005. Opportunity cost negative revenues in 2005, although slightly lower than 2004, nevertheless subtracted an estimated 4,126 travel-related service jobs from the US economy, concentrated in the restaurant, hotel, and hospitality industries.

---

13 * Excluding passenger fare receipts/exports.

Estimated 2005 US Travel-Related Service Job Loss ($ US Million)

(Sources: Runzheimer International 2005 Mobility Report and Institute for Research: Middle Eastern Policy, Inc.)

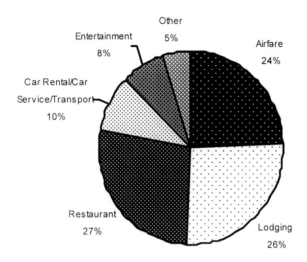

As painful as this loss of tourism revenues may be, a concerted effort to repair US visa policies could remedy the problem in the future. In the case of foreign student education visas, however, permanent damage has already been done to US-Arab relations.

5.0 Cutting America's Link to Tomorrow's Leaders

Arab student admissions into the US are still vastly below pre-9/11 levels, although F-1 (student) entries were on the upswing in 2005, according to Department of Homeland Security statistics. Quantitative analysis of admissions in 2005 seems to indicate that students from the Arab market are entering the US higher education system in higher numbers.

Arab Student Admissions into the United States[14]
(Source: Yearbook of Immigration Statistics, Department of Homeland Security)

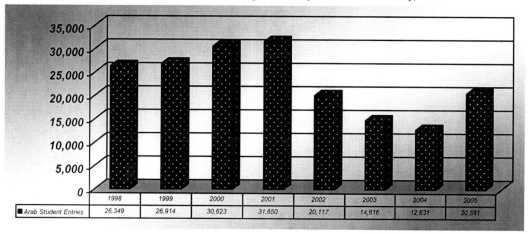

Arab Student Entries	1998	1999	2000	2001	2002	2003	2004	2005
	26,349	26,914	30,623	31,650	20,117	14,816	12,831	20,591

However, admission analysis alone leads to the wrong conclusions about enrollment levels in the 2004-2005 academic year. Greater numbers of student entries and exits in the year 2005 reflect the inefficiency of requiring students from key markets to return to their home countries (or a third country such as Mexico or Canada) to reapply for expiring education visas. This is because education visa (F-1) durations have been reduced for applicants originating in the Arab market. Citizens of 11 countries (accounting for 43% of Arab foreign students enrolled in 2001) no longer receive visas of sufficient duration to complete a four-year degree in the United States with normal entries and exits for home country visits.

---

14 Includes multiple entries

2005 Arab Student (F-1) Admissions into the United States [15]

(Source: Yearbook of Immigration Statistics, Department of Homeland Security)

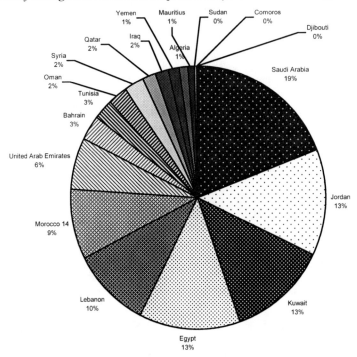

Students from markets undergoing rapid change and economic development, such as Libya, cannot obtain visas valid for more than one year. **In July of 2006, there was a backlog of 7,500 Saudi students waiting for visas to study in the US, according to the Saudi Ambassador to the United States.** [16]

---

15 Can include multiple entries by the same student.

16 The Value of a Visa? Priceless http://www.saudi-us-relations.org/articles/2006/interviews/060712-qunaibet-interview.html

Arab Student F-1 (Education) Visa Validity Periods
(Source: US State Department, August 2006)

Country	F-1 Visa Validity Period (Months)
Qatar, Lebanon, Kuwait, Jordan, Oman, Morocco, Bahrain, Tunisia, Egypt, Mauritania	60
United Arab Emirates	48
Palestine	36
Saudi Arabia, Syria	24
Yemen, Libya, Djibouti, Comoros, Algeria	12
Sudan	6
Somalia, Iraq	3

Some students who were enrolled in the US higher education system in 2001 returned to their home countries only to find themselves barred from reentry into the US. The degree of visa duration and reentry uncertainty has a direct effect on enrollment, as does the declining issuance rate of education visas. According to Institute for International Education (IIE) enrollment figures published in the annual "Open Doors" reports, the door has been slammed shut on Arab market students. 2004-2005 Arab enrollments declined 36% from the 2001-2002 level.

Arab Student Enrollment in US Higher Education by Academic Year
(Source: Institute for International Education)

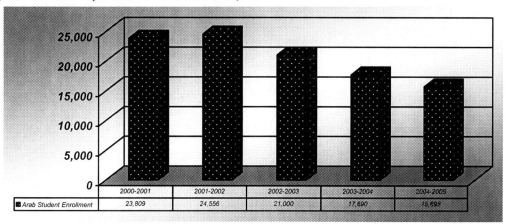

	2000-2001	2001-2002	2002-2003	2003-2004	2004-2005
■ Arab Student Enrollment	23,809	24,556	21,000	17,690	15,698

The economic and cultural impact of this decline in Arab student enrollment can only harm US interests in the long term. Currently, classrooms have many fewer Arab students offering their perspectives and contributing valuable research in US colleges and universities. Future generations of US business and government leaders will encounter fewer counterparts who understand or value the American system and the English language. Less important, though material, are the short-term economic impacts and losses for the higher education service industry.

International students brought $13.3 billion to the U.S. economy in money spent on tuition, living expenses, and related costs, according to the NAFSA: Association of International Educators. Using NAFSA's benchmark revenue per student, Arab students generated approximately $370 million dollars for the United States economy in the 2004-2005 academic year. Using publicly available benchmark input/out tables for revenues to employee headcount in the higher education industry, this number of foreign students supports approximately 4,296 direct higher education jobs.

Estimated US Revenues Generated by Arab Students, Best Case Scenario, Opportunity Cost ($ US Million)

(Source: Institute for Research: Middle Eastern Policy, Inc.)

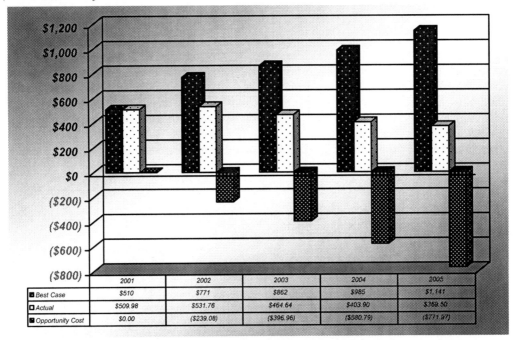

	2001	2002	2003	2004	2005
Best Case	$510	$771	$862	$985	$1,141
Actual	$509.98	$531.76	$464.64	$403.90	$369.50
Opportunity Cost	$0.00	($239.08)	($396.96)	($580.79)	($771.97)

In a best-case scenario where the US attempted to maintain this vital bridge to the Arab world, trend line enrollment could have reached 49,000 students from the region in 2005. The opportunity lost to the US higher education system is relevant: $1.989 billion and almost 9,000 additional higher education jobs.

*Recommendation #6: The US must reverse Arab student
declines through a two-part strategy. It must apply
sufficient additional visa processing resources to
accelerate the admission of qualified, credentialed
students from the region and reduce applicant backlogs. The
US must also bring in larger numbers of Arab students
through diversified scholarship grant distribution. Grants
should seek to increase the number of students from
countries that have historically sent few students to the
US.*

Fixing the Fulbright

The Fulbright Program is the preeminent US program for bringing foreign students into the US to study. The program began in the aftermath of World War II, when Senator J. William Fulbright led his peers in Congress and President Harry Truman in the search for ways to reduce international misunderstandings and global conflict. Fulbright correctly argued that exchanges of students, especially individuals likely to play future leadership roles in their country, would have a material impact on cross-cultural understanding, tolerance, and economic development. This vision led to the creation of a comprehensive program administered by the US State Department that was charged with building and rebuilding cultural bridges between nations.

A review of the year 2005 and historical Fulbright grants to foreign nationals in the Arab world reveals little State Department awareness of the need to build or rebuild bridges damaged by long-term neglect, 9/11, and tensions over US policies in the region. Scholarship grants to the future leaders of the US's largest regional import partner and key energy exporter, the UAE, were exactly zero in the 2004-2005 academic year. Saudi Arabia is in 14th place among the Arab League in terms of Fulbright grants from 1949-2004.

Fulbright Grants to Foreign Nationals
(Source: J. William Fulbright Foreign Scholarship Board Annual Report 2005)

Fulbright Grants	1949-2004	2005	Average Yearly
Egypt	1500	35	27
Morocco	913	36	17
Jordan	562	26	10
Palestine	527	25	10
Tunisia	424	40	8
Yemen	379	17	7
Syria	334	13	6
Lebanon	303	11	6
Sudan	235	0	4
Iraq	232	40	4
Oman	194	8	4
Algeria	188	8	3
Somalia	139	0	3
Saudi Arabia	87	14	2
Bahrain	57	13	1
Mauritania	27	0	0
United Arab Emirates	24	0	0
Djibouti	12	0	0
Libya	11	0	0
Qatar	11	1	0
Kuwait	9	3	0

While most year 2005 country grants are above historical annual levels, they do not reflect the "rebuilding bridges" objective that lies at the core of the Fulbright program's mission.

The government of Saudi Arabia has sought to rebuild bridges through a new program offering 15,000 scholarships for students to study in the US. 10,229 Saudi students registered for the 2006-2007 academic year will receive scholarships of up to $30,000 per year. US government officials are now working to ensure that all 15,000 students have visas to enter by January 2007.[17]

---

17 New program sends 15,000 Saudis to U.S. colleges, Chicago Sun - Times. Sep 10, 2006. p. A27

*Recommendation #7: The US State Department and Fulbright
Foreign Scholarship Board should double the number of Arab
scholarship grants and reprioritize their distribution
toward countries whose trade potential and regional
influence has not historically been reflected in Fulbright
allotments. Grant distribution criteria should aim to
attract worthy scholars from historically underrepresented
countries like the UAE and Libya where no foreign student
recovery program (like Saudi Arabia's) currently exists.*

6.0 Country-Level Damage Assessment

The following subsections provide a country-level trade damage assessment, insights about the US visa process, case studies, and additional recommendations for Arab countries typically importing more than US$1 billion in merchandise from the US.

United Arab Emirates

In 2005, the UAE emerged as the Arab market's largest US merchandise importer. The UAE is now a top priority for US consulate service innovation and process streamlining. The Department of State, the U.S. Embassy in Abu Dhabi, and the Consulate General in Dubai implemented a mandatory Electronic Visa Application Form (EVAF) on March 1, 2006. The EVAF allows visa applicants to fill out their applications on the Internet to expedite visa interviews and processing; visa clerks and counselor service personnel no longer need to manually enter visa application data.[18]

The consulate in Dubai also dropped required appointments for applicants seeking student visas and emergency medical cases, and will take applications on a walk-in basis.

UAE Opportunity Cost Summary
(Source: Institute for Research: Middle Eastern Policy, Inc.)

	2005 Actual	2005 Best Case	Opportunity Cost
Jobs Created in the US	63,619	81,260	-17,641
Total US Merchandise Exports (billion)	$8.5	$10.8	-$2.3
Total US Market Share	14%	18%	-4%

Although filling out the EVAF application online does cut processing time, it does not mean the application has been transmitted to the embassy or consulate for processing. The application must still be printed out and display a proprietary barcode. This paper application can then be brought to the Consular Section on the scheduled interview day.

---

18 US Fed News Service, Feb 14, 2006.

Recommendation #8: Currently, the EVAF is cutting data entry overhead in the consulate, but does not deliver added time savings for visa applicants. The EVAF needs to arrive at a development stage in which successful data transmission initiates back-office visa processing, particularly security reviews, and cuts overall application processing time.

The Dubai Ports World Debacle

Late in 2005, news of a potential $6.8 billion[19] acquisition of the British shipper Peninsular & Oriental Steam Navigation Co. (P&O) by Dubai Ports World (DPW) began circulating in the Asian and British press. Few American observers realized that a successful DPW takeover would make this government-owned firm the top port operator in the world and place the management of six key American ports into the hands of DPW. Beginning in October of 2005, US representatives of the 12 departments and agencies that make up the Committee on Foreign Investment in the United States (CFIUS) investigated the potential acquisition with support from the intelligence community and the Departments of Transportation and Energy.

CFIUS was created in 1975 to review sensitive foreign investments, and its member agencies include the National Security Council, Department of Treasury (Chair), State Department, Department of Defense, Justice Department, Department of Commerce, and Department of Homeland Security, as well as the National Economic Council, United States Trade Representative, Office of Management and Budget, Council of Economic Advisors, and Office of Science and Technology Policy. The Departments of Energy and Transportation and other U.S. agencies participate in transaction reviews that fall within their jurisdictions.

Actual US Merchandise Exports to UAE, Best Case Scenario, Opportunity Cost ($ US Billion)

(Source: Institute for Research: Middle Eastern Policy, Inc.)

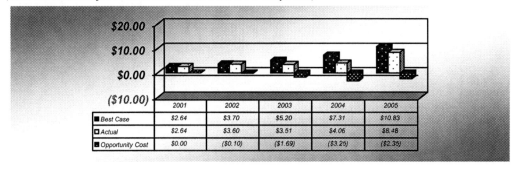

	2001	2002	2003	2004	2005
■ Best Case	$2.64	$3.70	$5.20	$7.31	$10.83
□ Actual	$2.64	$3.60	$3.51	$4.06	$8.48
■ Opportunity Cost	$0.00	($0.10)	($1.69)	($3.25)	($2.35)

---

19 West at risk of losing oil money Gulf states turn to Asia for growth MARKETPLACE by Bloomberg:[3 Edition]

James Cordahi and James Hertling. International Herald Tribune Paris:Jan 30, 2006. p. 14

The 2006 congressional opposition to DPW's acquisition of P&O may determine the future of large-scale direct investment in critical US infrastructure by foreign investors. As in the 1970s, investors from petroleum-exporting states are again scouring foreign markets to invest revenues generated from higher oil prices in attractive overseas investments. Foreign direct investment is not the only economic factor at stake: the "ripple effect" of a deteriorating business climate could curtail pending export deals affecting tens of thousands of US manufacturing jobs. **Getting into the US through efficient visa processes is the first step in trade and investment. Avoiding unwarranted opposition to large deals through false "national security" or other barriers is the second.**

In November of 2005, Emirates Air ordered 42 Boeing 777 jets at a value of up to $9.7 billion according to Boeing list prices—Boeing's largest order for the aircraft.[20] Emirates Air will receive one 777 airliner per month over the next five years. Far from being a passive customer, UAE also requested that Boeing build a larger 300-passenger version of the futuristic new 787 Dreamliner, giving it a future purchase alternative to Europe's Airbus A350. **Efficient bilateral non-immigrant exits and entries allow large purchases like this one to be signed, sealed, and delivered.**

Arab entities are not the only investors watching the US visa and investment climate. The US trade deficit reached $725.75 billion in 2005. Chinese and Indian investors with capital generated from merchandise and service trade surpluses are also seeking higher-yielding direct investments in the United States.[21]

Politics vs. National Security Concerns

In 2005, overseas investors witnessed a growing protectionist movement fueled by US lobbyists attempting to scuttle "hostile" foreign acquisitions through dubious claims of "national security" concerns. China's third-largest state-owned oil company, CNOOC, attempted to buy Unocal for $18.5 billion by outbidding Chevron in 2005. Members of the US House of Representatives voted 398-15 for a non-binding resolution against the purchase, stating that the takeover "would threaten to impair the national security of the United States." [22] Lawmakers who wanted to see Unocal in Chevron's hands found it both easier and more effective to raise the red herring of national security concerns and deter an energy-hungry China from scooping up global reserves through acquisition than to deal with the more mundane merits of the deal.

Interested parties in the Port of Miami deployed the very same strategy. As reported by the Wall Street Journal in February 2006, the Dubai Ports takeover of P&O received almost no

---

20 Emirates has Boeing, Airbus competing for big sale:[Third Edition]

Lauren Villagran, The Associated Press. St. Louis Post - Dispatch St. Louis, Mo.:Apr 27, 2006. p. B.4

21 U.S. assets entice buyers; Dollar-rich nations like China, India seek to recycle wealth

Bernard Wysocki Jr. and Michael M. Phillips. Wall Street Journal (Europe). Brussels:Feb 23, 2006. p. 8

22 US lawmakers meddle in CNOOC's Unocal bid http://www.chinadaily.com.cn/english/doc/2005-07/06/content_457677.htm

attention on Capitol Hill or in the US media until lobbyists from a disgruntled stevedore operation based in Ft. Lauderdale began to brief key lawmakers about "national security" issues. An Eller & Company subsidiary called Continental Stevedoring & Terminals Inc. manages terminals in the Port of Miami contracted through a partnership with P&O. Long before DPW began bidding for P&O, Continental was locked in a fierce legal battle with the port operator, alleging that P&O was trying to "muscle in" on Continental's portion of the operations. This commercial dispute led to a lawsuit that the Eller subsidiary filed including a few new pages citing US "national security" concerns. Eller & Co's highly technical commercial lawsuits filed in the US and UK on February 17th, 2006 sought "to rectify egregious breaches of fiduciary duty, self-dealing and concealment of material facts" on the part of Dubai Ports' acquisition target, P&O. [23]

Seeing an advantage in packaging its commercial grievance within a Trojan horse of "national security", Eller & Co. lawyers from the firm of Bilzin Sumberg sprinkled quotes from the 9/11 Commission and investigating agencies throughout their 52-page filing, which states that "several of the hijackers" passed through the United Arab Emirates en route to the United States. The lawsuit claims that stevedore Continental didn't want "to become involuntarily a business partner with the government of Dubai," although the majority of the legal filing deals with Continental's longstanding commercial complaints against P&O.

Eller & Co. lobbyists received attention on Capitol Hill. Connecticut attorney Alan Neigher, who helped craft the Eller lobbying initiative, gave lawmakers two messages, but emphasized the last: **"We thought the purchase of P&O was a very bad idea. It endangered our operations in Miami….It raised enormous questions about port security -- and still does."** Many prominent lawmakers, from Bob Menendez to Hillary Clinton and Charles Schumer, were receptive to the national security issue and opposed the DPW deal while crafting legislation seeking to stop it. The national security issue framework driven by a commercial dispute came to dominate all aspects of debate over the DPW acquisition in Congress and the news media. According to Sen. Charles Schumer's spokesman, Israel Klein, the Eller & Co grievance "was really the canary in the mineshaft for many people on the Hill and in the media."

---

23 Small Florida Firm Sowed Seed of Port Dispute; Eller's Suits and Lob Lie Behind Dubai Furor; Approval Delayed in U.K.

Neil King Jr. and Greg Hitt. Wall Street Journal (Eastern Edition). New York, N.Y.:Feb 28, 2006. p. A.3

Bowing to pressure from Congress, on February 26, 2006, DPW requested a second CFIUS review of a restructured transaction placing control of US ports into a US entity.[24] The blockage of DPW's acquisition of US ports is viewed as a setback by many prominent analysts. Anthony Shadid of the Washington Post summarizes it as "a failure of Dubai officials to market themselves and master public relations."[25] Overseas, many focused on probable outcomes for bilateral investment. Naguib Sawiris of Eqypt's telecom multinational Orascom stated to the Financial Times, "This could hinder US firms who want to do acquisitions in the Middle East. You know, if you don't allow us, we won't allow you."[26] Others, including IRmep, view DPW's acquisition as a call to action in an effort that has only just begun.

DPW Analysis and Lessons Learned

From Yemen to the UK, DPW's record on investment in operations, modernization, and commitment to safety, security, and efficiency is world-class. Concerns that the UAE is not aligned with US national security initiatives have been driven by disinformation and misrepresentation of the UAE's longstanding support for US naval bases, supply, and logistics.

UAE ports host more U.S. Navy ships than any port outside the United States.

> "The UAE provides outstanding support for the U.S. Navy at the ports of Jebel Ali - which is managed by DP World - and Fujairah and for the U.S. Air Force at al Dhafra Air Base (tankers and surveillance and reconnaissance aircraft). The UAE also hosts the UAE Air Warfare Center, the leading fighter training center in the Middle East. Joint air force exercises between GCC countries and the United States and other Western allies take place regularly in the UAE." -White House Statement[27]

---

24 Committee On Foreign Investment In The United States Welcomes Dubai Ports World's Announcement To Submit To New Review

US Fed News Service, Including US State News Washington, D.C.:Feb 26, 2006. p. n/a

25 The Towering Dream of Dubai:[FINAL Edition]

Anthony Shadid. The Washington Post Washington, D.C.:Apr 30, 2006. p. A01

26 Ports Backlash Makes Arab Investors Wary William Wallis. The Financial Times .:Mar 1, 2006.

27 http://www.whitehouse.gov/news/releases/2006/02/20060222-10.html

US Merchandise Manufactures Exports to UAE by Industry Job Creation

(Source: Institute for Research: Middle Eastern Policy, Inc.)

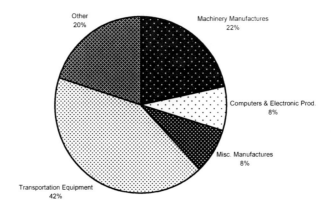

In hindsight, proper pre-acquisition due diligence and disclosure on the part of Peninsular & Oriental Steam Navigation Co. could have resulted in a vastly different outcome. DPW could have been alerted to the potential Miami conflagration with Continental Stevedoring and moved to redress the real underlying commercial issues jeopardizing the acquisition, to the satisfaction of all parties.

Continental was able to whip up a constituency motivated by a destructive "faux" national security issue. America's real stakeholders in US-Arab trade deployed late, on highly unfavorable ground. With proper resources and early warning, a broader array of US-Arab trade constituencies would have begun working on Capitol Hill in October 2005 before major issues around the acquisition were framed and circulated by detractors. National security, economic development, and fighting violent extremism abroad, properly framed, are all issues that just as easily could have propelled a full acquisition, rather than sinking it.

The DPW affair also highlighted the glaring absence of an effective caucus on Capitol Hill. There are over 150 caucuses and other Congressional membership organizations covering nearly every subject, policy, and geographic region, but none are focused specifically on US-Arab trade and economic prosperity. The one that comes closest is the Congressional Middle East Economic Partnership Caucus, which was formed on February 15, 2006, co-chaired by Reps. Phil English (R-PA), Paul Ryan (R-WI), Darrell Issa (R-CA), William Jefferson (D-LA), Gregory Meeks (D-NY), and Ben Chandler (D-KY). Caucuses are important in the House of Representatives because they allow interested members and their staff to work together on critical constituent issues, promote effective legislative agendas, and fight legislation or political subterfuge that can damage US interests. Caucus members often join together to introduce legislation, influence their colleagues and key government officials, and make floor speeches to drive issues related to the caucus's mission.

A more focused "US-Arab Trade and Economic Prosperity Caucus" devoted to proactively avoiding future foreign investment snafus would be chaired by members with the highest economic stake in US-Arab trade: Texas, Washington, California, and Ohio. The caucus should be charged with maintaining already high capital goods and services exports to the region while facilitating efficient recycling of petroleum dollars back into the US economy through foreign direct investment.

The tide of "national security" hype that slowed the DPW acquisition of US port management is turning. Inchcape Shipping Services is a UK-based corporation providing shipping agency services for over 50,000 annual vessel arrivals and departures at 200 ports around the world, including more than 24 in the US. Inchape was acquired in January 2006 by a Dubai-government-owned corporation, Istithmar PJSC.

On April 28, 2006, President Bush approved a $1.2 billion Dubai acquisition of U.S. plants that make precision-engineered airfoils and military components for the Department of Defense. This allows Dubai International Capital, LLC to assume control of nine factories located in the United States that were formerly run by UK-based Doncasters Group Ltd. Dubai Ports World became the first global transport company to obtain a rigorous international security certification: "As a consequence of DP World's adoption and implementation of the standard, its network of ports will have the ability to effectively implement mechanisms and processes to address any security vulnerabilities at strategic and operational levels, as well as establish preventive action plans." According to a DPW press release, Ian Hodgskinson, director of the certification organization LRQA, said, "This is an important step in securing the supply chain globally. It is a challenging standard to achieve and we have been impressed with the rigorous effort DP World has put in to achieve it. We look forward to other leaders in the industry embracing the standard."

Recommendation #9: The failed DPW acquisition reveals that interested parties can successfully orchestrate negative campaigns based on false "national security" issues raised by domestic competitors. This raises the possibility of similar false alarms raised by foreign intelligence services. CIA and FBI security visa application security reviews that draw upon foreign source intelligence should not rely on sources that are Arab market rivals or competitors: bad intelligence leads to visa rejection and drives a wedge between the US and key Arab business leaders.

Saudi Arabia

Saudi Arabia has historically been the most important US trading and energy partner in the region. Saudi Arabia generated 60,269 direct and indirect manufacturing-related jobs in the United States in the year 2005 and $6.8 billion in export revenues for the US.

Saudi Arabia Opportunity Cost Summary
(Source: Institute for Research: Middle Eastern Policy, Inc.)

	2005 Actual	2005 Best Case	Opportunity Cost
Jobs Created in the US	60,269	158,595	-98,326
Total Merchandise Imports from the US (billion)	$6.8	$18.0	-$11.2
Total US Market Share	15.2%	40%	-24.8%

Under the best-case scenario, US exports of manufactured goods to Saudi Arabia would have reached $18 billion in the year 2005 (a 40% import market share similar to the US export relationship with Mexico) and supported 158,595 manufacturing-related jobs. However, the visitor flow vital for facilitating higher levels of trade did not significantly recover through 2005.

Direct and Indirect Manufacturing Jobs Generated by Saudi Arabia in the US
Source: Institute for Research: Middle Eastern Policy, Inc.

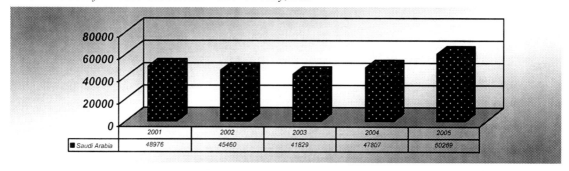

The growing visa trade barrier has had a particular impact on Saudi business travelers who have fallen into visa renewal "limbo." One Saudi business traveler, the chairman of a large commercial group who received an MBA and engineering degrees from US universities in the early 1990s, can no longer personally source equipment or professional services from the United States. After submitting a visa renewal application on December 2002 in Riyadh, he received a series of excuses in communications from the US consular section:

1. **Initial response: No current approval to issue a visa – would advise of permission if granted.**

2. **February 2002: Consulate reports "staff shortage" and requests passport number to advise of future visa status.**
3. **August 2003: Consulate reports continued "staff shortage" and lack of control over process.**
4. **October 2004: Consulate reports that the non-immigrant visa application has now expired after one year.**
5. **December 5, 2005: He reapplies for a visa. Application expires.**
6. **March 2006: He reapplies for a visa.**
7. **July 2006: Consulate informs him that his application is being processed in Washington, DC and that he will be informed of any status change.**

The series of email responses submitted by this business traveler demonstrate that in addition to visa issuance or rejection after long processing times, there is now a third de facto status for applicants: "limbo."

"Limbo Letter" from the US Consulate in Riyadh
(Source: Institute for Research: Middle Eastern Policy, Inc.)

From:	Cons, Riyadh - (Visitors Visas) [RiyadhNIV@state.gov]
Sent:	December, 2005
To:	
Subject:	RE: US Visa Application Status
Follow Up Flag:	Follow up
Flag Status:	Flagged

Your visa application is still being processed. We will notify you once we are able to issue your visa.

Thanks.

2005: A Year of Missed Opportunities

Higher energy prices and increased purchasing power aren't the only factors fueling higher import demand in Saudi Arabia. Saudi Arabia's accession to the WTO in 2005 has led to generally lower import tariffs. After WTO accession, 63% of merchandise categories are capped at the 10-20% rate band and 53 categories will see lower tariffs.

WTO has also opened a number of key service industries to foreign investment for the first time. Contingents of foreign and Saudi investors are meeting to craft cross-border service providers' market entry deals. Major sectors with joint ventures and foreign investors moving into the market include life insurance, reinsurance, banking, and health insurance. Liberalization of the financial markets has led to many new entrants and expansions. Citibank is seeking a license to reenter the market after selling its share of Saudi American Bank two years ago. Amex Saudi Arabia Ltd. is executing a card acceptance growth strategy to increase the number of merchants in the network. Although these services are ideally provided "in-market," in 2006 and 2007 new market entrants will determine leadership in service industries. **Visa delays affecting negotiations taking place in financial and insurance centers such as New York will drive many to London for joint ventures and mergers and acquisitions advice.**

New demand across other industries is creating unprecedented export opportunities that US manufacturers are, for the most part, losing to foreign competitors:

New regional airline startups: National and startup airlines are diversifying their jetliners. SAMA, National Air Services $400 million jetliner purchase: Timeframe: 3-5 years.

Defense initiatives: Saudi Arabia is forming a new helicopter brigade, awarding contracts for two jet fighter platforms for the Saudi Royal Air Force, and upgrading its National Guard and border security system. Timeframe: 5-10 years. Total estimated value: $104 billion.

Energy infrastructure: Saudi Arabia is investing in new production capacity, including offshore rigs. Timeframe: 5-10 years. Total estimated value: $80 billion.

Economic cities: Saudi Arabia is constructing entirely new cities, such as Tabuk Economic City, King Abdullah Economic City, Prince Abdul Aziz bin Musaed Economic City, and the Riyadh Financial District Hospital. Entrepreneurs are competing for construction tenders as well as hotel franchise and residential complex construction contracts. Timeframe: 2007-2012. Total estimated value: $77 billion.

Electric power: Demand is increasing by 5.5% annually; $117 billion investment needed over the next 20 years.

Water infrastructure: Investments of $100 billion ($43 billion for desalinization) are reaching tender stage, including a 2007 Riyadh water contract and 2008 Jeddah dam projects.

US visa restrictions will hit new service industry joint ventures harder than merchandise trade, since mobility of human capital for training, strategy meetings, facilities tours, and continuing education requires efficient and dependable visa processing.

US Merchandise Exports to Saudi Arabia, Best Case Scenario, Opportunity Cost ($ US Billion)
(Source: Institute for Research: Middle Eastern Policy, Inc.)

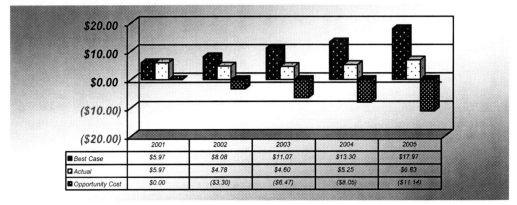

	2001	2002	2003	2004	2005
■ Best Case	$5.97	$8.08	$11.07	$13.30	$17.97
□ Actual	$5.97	$4.78	$4.60	$5.25	$6.83
■ Opportunity Cost	$0.00	($3.30)	($6.47)	($8.05)	($11.14)

The hardest hit merchandise industries in terms of real employment and export revenues over the past four years include processed food products (-35.6%), beverage and tobacco products (-63.5%), non-apparel textile products (-53.3%), and furniture and related products (-61.5%).

US Merchandise Manufactures Exports to Saudi Arabia by Industry Job Creation
(Source: Institute for Research: Middle Eastern Policy, Inc.)

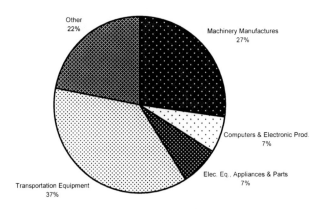

Visa restrictions have hit Saudi students harder than students from elsewhere in the Arab market. Assistant Secretary of State C. David Welch summed up the issue in a March 30, 2006 interview:[28]

> "It was disappointing to me the low number of Saudi students in the United States. I think King Abdullah has taken a look at that himself and said this is a situation we would like to rectify and is willing to contribute resources to that end. So that we don't end up with a situation, ten, fifteen, twenty years down the road where we take a look at the Saudi cabinet of the day and we don't see people like we see today -- like Prince Turki for example, who had been educated in the United States, like Prince Saud, who had been educated in the United States. Those are links that are enormously beneficial for us in cultivating the kind of relationships needed to succeed in our foreign policy objectives there, but also enormously beneficial for Saudis in bringing to development in the kingdom some of the experience that they gain here in America."

Mishandling diplomats and dignitaries visiting on diplomatic passports can also effectively rule out US bidders on major government sponsored regional infrastructure projects. One member of Saudi Arabia's consultative council underscored the cost of undiplomatic treatment.

> "Every time I've returned to the US, even with a diplomatic passport, I've been taken aside and grilled by Homeland Security. I'm there on official business, and am treated like dirt. I am not going again, ever." **Member of the Majlis Ash Shura**

---

28 A Conversation with Assistant Secretary of State

C. David Welch http://www.saudi-us-relations.org/articles/2006/interviews/060330-welch-interview-complete.html

Egypt

US-Egypt trade relations have suffered the visa trade barrier fallout. In spite of spiraling demand, the US market share of Egyptian imports, which should approach the 30% levels the US enjoyed in the late 1990s, remains stagnant.

US Merchandise Exports to Egypt, Best Case Scenario, Opportunity Cost ($ US Billion)
(Source: Institute for Research: Middle Eastern Policy, Inc.)

	2005 Actual	2005 Best Case	Opportunity Cost
Jobs Created in the US	20,993	46,167	-25,234
Total US Merchandise Exports (billion)	$3.2	$7.0	-$3.8
Total US Market Share	13.2%	29.0%	-15.8%

As in the UAE, visa processing facilities in Egypt have gone digital—a vast improvement over previous processing systems. Non-immigrant applicants for business and tourist visas can now access the US consulate in Cairo for updates on visa processing times via the Internet.

Actual US Merchandise Exports to Egypt, Best Case Scenario, Opportunity Cost ($ US Billion)
(Source: Institute for Research: Middle Eastern Policy, Inc.)

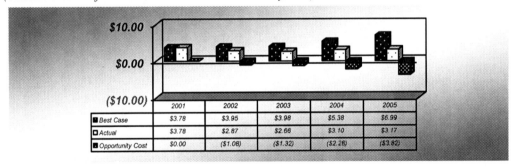

	2001	2002	2003	2004	2005
Best Case	$3.78	$3.95	$3.98	$5.38	$6.99
Actual	$3.78	$2.87	$2.66	$3.10	$3.17
Opportunity Cost	$0.00	($1.08)	($1.32)	($2.28)	($3.82)

In late August 2006, the Cairo embassy was notifying potential visa applicants of a historically low two-week waiting time between application and initial interview.

"Wait times for U.S. visa appointment are at a record low: The wait time for a Non-immigrant Visa interview at the U.S. Embassy is the lowest it has been in two years. If you call today, you will get an appointment in two weeks. The waiting time constantly changes, depending on demand, so it will vary depending on when you call. But as of today, it is only two weeks.[29]"

Egypt Non-Immigrant Visa Processing Durations
(Source: US Consulate in Egypt)

Nonimmigrant Visa Interview Appointment	Calendar Days
Visitor's Visa	18
Student/Exchange Visitor's Visa *** (Excludes A, G, K, and V)	1
Typical Processing Wait Time	2
Special Clearance Administrative Processing	30

Kuwait

US-Kuwait trade has fallen below its potential despite generally productive relations since the first Gulf War. Total Kuwaiti non-immigrant entries to the US slipped from 14,060 in 2000 to 11,080 in 2005.

US Merchandise Exports to Kuwait, Best Case Scenario, Opportunity Cost ($ US Billion)
(Source: Institute for Research: Middle Eastern Policy, Inc.)

	2005 Actual	2005 Best Case	Opportunity Cost
Jobs Created in the US	18,713	23,183	-4,470
Total US Merchandise Exports (billion)	$2.0	$2.5	-$0.5
Total US Market Share	16%	20%	-4%

Growth patterns similar to those of the larger petroleum-producing states have created Kuwaiti demand for US industrial machinery and energy-production-related education services. However, the experience of Kuwaiti mechanical engineering doctoral student Saleh al Hajiri reveals that students holding the proper visa cannot always count on finishing their studies in the United States. Hajiri began his studies in the year 2000. During the final week of August 2006, he was arrested and deported from the United States and his student visa was canceled on charges of "suspicion."

---

29 US Embassy in Cairo http://cairo.usembassy.gov/consular.htm#nvs

Actual US Merchandise Exports to Kuwait, Best Case Scenario, Opportunity Cost ($ US Billion)

(Source: Institute for Research: Middle Eastern Policy, Inc.)

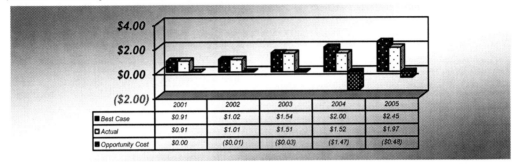

	2001	2002	2003	2004	2005
■ Best Case	$0.91	$1.02	$1.54	$2.00	$2.45
□ Actual	$0.91	$1.01	$1.51	$1.52	$1.97
■ Opportunity Cost	$0.00	($0.01)	($0.03)	($1.47)	($0.48)

DHS's suspicions did not prevent them from allowing Hajiri to fly from New York, where he was first detained, to Los Angeles with temporary documents in order to attend a September 19, 2006 appointment to discuss his presence in the US. [30]

Hajiri attended the meeting, but four days later, five police officers arrived at his home to take Hajiri, his wife, and their four children to the Los Angeles airport for twelve more hours of interrogation. Hajiri's visa was cancelled and he was told to leave the US. His five-year-old son Hamad, born in the United States, was allowed to stay.

Cases such as Hajiri's create a wave of uncertainty and doubt that ripples back to his home country and diminishes what should be one of the strongest US relationships in the region.

---

30 Kuwaiti student latest victim of racial profiling http://archive.gulfnews.com/articles/06/08/30/10063701.html

Algeria

Algeria's race to develop energy infrastructure has the nation looking for increased investment and trade. Currently, Iran is winning market share in Algeria as the US continues to squeeze access to its markets for Algerian industrial buyers. Non-immigrant entries from Algeria reached 6,017 in 2001, but fell by half to only 3,023 in 2005.

US Merchandise Exports to Algeria, Best Case Scenario, Opportunity Cost ($ US Billion)

(Source: Institute for Research: Middle Eastern Policy, Inc.)

	2005 Actual	2005 Best Case	Opportunity Cost
Jobs Created in the US	5,370	13,027	-7,657
Total US Merchandise Exports (billion)	$1.2	$2.82	-$1.85
Total US Market Share	5%	12.5%	-7.5%

Over half of Algeria's current imports from the US are concentrated in industrial machinery (53%), sourced primarily from Texas and Louisiana.

Actual US Merchandise Exports to Algeria, Best Case Scenario, Opportunity Cost ($ US Billion)

(Source: Institute for Research: Middle Eastern Policy, Inc.)

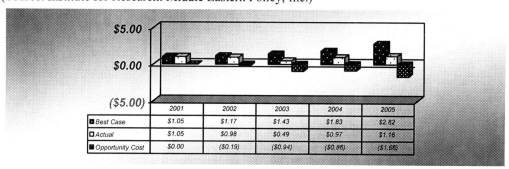

	2001	2002	2003	2004	2005
Best Case	$1.05	$1.17	$1.43	$1.83	$2.82
Actual	$1.05	$0.98	$0.49	$0.97	$1.16
Opportunity Cost	$0.00	($0.19)	($0.94)	($0.86)	($1.66)

Closing the door on Algerian non-immigrant travelers needlessly throws away an opportunity to expand US influence in an up-and-coming energy producer state, leaving trade and investment squarely within the Iranian sphere of influence.[31]

---

31 Algeria calls for Iran investment in growing economy http://www.mehrnews.ir/en/NewsDetail.aspx?NewsID=382218

Qatar

Qatar, with a population of only 885,000, serves as an important regional communications hub in the Arabian Gulf. An important energy exporter, Qatar also looks to the US for high-value-added industrial manufactures such as jet engines, aircraft, and transportation equipment for its air service.

US Merchandise Exports to Qatar, Best Case Scenario, Opportunity Cost ($ US Billion)
(Source: Institute for Research: Middle Eastern Policy, Inc.)

	2005 Actual	2005 Best Case	Opportunity Cost
Jobs Created in the US	10,745	21,924	11,179
Total US Merchandise Exports (billion)	$1.0	$2.01	$1.01
Total US Market Share	14.7%	30%	15.3%

Qatar's non-immigrant entries in the US fell from 2,344 in the year 2001 to 1,391 in 2005 in spite of Qatar's accommodating a critical repositioning of US forces in the region in 2002. Qatar received US forces at the Al-Udeid air base after they were forced to leave the Prince Sultan air base in Saudi Arabia.

Actual US Merchandise Exports to Qatar, Best Case Scenario, Opportunity Cost ($ US Billion)
(Source: Institute for Research: Middle Eastern Policy, Inc.)

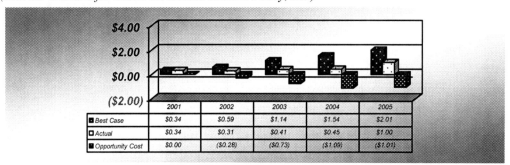

	2001	2002	2003	2004	2005
Best Case	$0.34	$0.59	$1.14	$1.54	$2.01
Actual	$0.34	$0.31	$0.41	$0.45	$1.00
Opportunity Cost	$0.00	($0.28)	($0.73)	($1.09)	($1.01)

US-Qatar relations are important, but have been hampered by low visitor flow. During a time when Qatar occupied a non-permanent seat on the US Security Council and ramped up global reporting from the Qatar-based Al-Jazeerah satellite channel, increased visitor flow would have buoyed mutual understanding and trade opportunities.

Iraq

The US invasion and occupation of Iraq and investment in massive new US embassy facilities there has not improved non-immigrant visitor flow from Iraq to the US. Non-immigrant entries in the Saddam Hussein era through 2001 were substantially higher (2,263) than the highly restricted year 2005 non-immigrant entries (1,459).

US Merchandise Exports to Iraq, Best Case Scenario, Opportunity Cost ($ US Billion)

(Source: Institute for Research: Middle Eastern Policy, Inc.)

	2005 Actual	2005 Best Case	Opportunity Cost
Jobs Created in the US	11,007	18,837	-7,830
Total US Merchandise Exports (billion)	$1.37	$2.35	-$1.0
Total US Market Share	7.0%	12.0%	-5.0%

Currently, the US Embassy in Baghdad only accepts applications for three types of non-immigrant visas:

Diplomatic and government officials
Representatives to international organizations
US government funded exchange visitors

All other non-immigrant and immigrant visa applications must be filed at another US Embassy or Consulate outside of Iraq.[32] The US effectively remains "walled off" for Iraqi students desiring a US education. In the 2000-2001 academic year, 155 Iraqi students were enrolled and studying in the US, according to the IIE. In the 2004-2005 academic year, there were only 142.

---

32 US Embassy in Baghdad http://iraq.usembassy.gov/iraq/consular.html

Actual US Merchandise Exports to Iraq, Best Case Scenario, Opportunity Cost ($ US Billion)

(Source: Institute for Research: Middle Eastern Policy, Inc.)

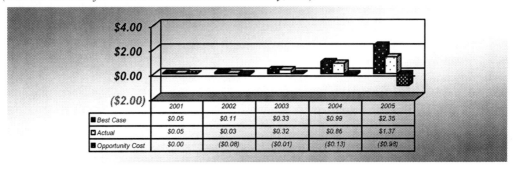

	2001	2002	2003	2004	2005
Best Case	$0.05	$0.11	$0.33	$0.99	$2.35
Actual	$0.05	$0.03	$0.32	$0.86	$1.37
Opportunity Cost	$0.00	($0.08)	($0.01)	($0.13)	($0.98)

7.0 Conclusions: Restoring Visitors and Trade

Restoring Arab non-immigrant entries and annual visitor growth to pre-9/11 levels is in the US national interest. However candid interview responses from business leaders in the most affected nation, Saudi Arabia, reveal the cumulative effect of five years of visa restrictions. Even if Arab business and diplomatic leaders as well as scholars could get through the visa gauntlet, many are now less willing to try, citing huge changes in treatment at ports of entry.

> "It has changed a lot! Before 9/11 I used to wish to travel to the US every year. After 9/11, I wish I don't have to! I've been to the US three times before the 9/11. None after. My personal travel hasn't been changed. Except that the US isn't in my destination list anymore, and I really hope and wish I won't need to have it back on the list again! Not even for my dependants." **Mohammed al-Misehal, VP of Al-Misehal Telecommunications, Riyadh**

The shift away from US sourced merchandise and services clearly benefits one region's economy in particular: the Far East.

> "Well, maybe our business will shift to Europe, China and Far East in general. (We will pick up new languages). When you knock my door several times (looking for business or providing one) and no one is answering the door in a reasonable time, you tend to go somewhere else." **Nabeel Al Mojil, Dammam, Saudi Arabia**

The new US willingness to accept massive trade deficits while closing the door to visas that facilitate American service and merchandise exports perpetuates a negative feedback loop. According to Georgetown University's Jean-Francois Seznec this adds to the Arab market's eastward search for imports and financial services.

> "…but the real tangible activity, both diplomatically and economically, is increasingly with China. The Saudis are more eager to be friends with the lender states, Japan and China, than to actually support a US government that is kept financially afloat by, and thus dependent on, the far eastern powers."[33]

Fond personal memories and proactive scholarship programs may induce generations of graduates to send their children for a US education, but an added stimulus is missing for reigniting US-Arab market business.

> "But maybe next year when my son graduates from high school. I will contact a few universities in my home town Portland, Oregon and see how it goes. I still have faith on the USA I know, not the current one! **Nabeel Al Mojil, Dammam, Saudi Arabia**

---

33 Doubtful of the US, Saudi Arabia begins looking east By Jean-Francois Seznec http://www.saudi-us-relations.org/articles/2006/ioi/060928-seznec-east.html

Former visitors also mention perceived anti-Arab bigotry, discrimination and treatment as a suspected criminal as reason enough for avoiding all travel to the US:

> "The US government has given its ....media to convince the majority of the US citizens with loads and loads of fake stories and myths about the Muslims in general and Saudis in particular. Also, we hear from many friends, the experiences they've went through in the US airports as soon as they reach the immigration desk. They treat many of them like if they were criminals! Why would I subject my self for all this hassle? Why would I subject my self to be verbally or especially harmed in the street or being indirectly or directly humiliated and insulted in the immigration office or by the FBI?! **Mohammed al-Misehal, VP of Al-Misehal Telecommunications, Riyadh**

The quantitative and qualitative damage assessment in this report reveal real problems that cannot be redressed through public relations campaigns or expressions of concern by US government officials. Cutting the negative feedback reverberating through US-Arab market relations requires real policy changes. American stakeholders will know recommended actions have been implemented when, once again, non-immigrant Arab visitor entry growth returns to pre-9/11 levels. Few policy decisions can be as easily evaluated as non-immigrant visits. Plummeting visits and stagnating US-Arab trade due to denial or under-funded security review processes must not be allowed to continue.

Appendix - Opportunity Cost Methodology

Travel and Tourism

Utilizing average international traveler expenditures in the US taken from surveys conducted by the US Office of Travel and Tourism Industries for the Middle East and country-specific visitor counts from the Department of Homeland Security, IRmep calculates the total revenues from passengers originating in each Arab country. Our "best-case" benchmark assumes continued arithmetic visitor trends (positive, or in a few cases, negative) based on pre-9/11 trends.

Arab Students

Utilizing the Institute for International Education (IIE) "origin of student" statistics and estimated mean revenue per student, IRmep calculates total student revenues on a per-country basis. Our "best-case" scenario assumes continued arithmetic student growth based on pre-9/11 trends. For education industry direct job creation estimates, IRmep compiles an "input/output" table using benchmark higher education entities that report their annual revenues and employee headcount.

Arab Market Imports from the US

Utilizing the US Census Bureau foreign trade statistics, total country import figures from the CIA, and national accounts reporting to the IMF and World Bank, IRmep calculates what "share" of total foreign country merchandise imports are supplied by the US to each Arab country. IRmep then constructs a "best-case" market scenario share percentage estimate based on historical data, benchmark import market share with comparable countries and addressable market and estimated share growth trend continuance in a goodwill trade environment.

Direct and Indirect Manufacturing-Related US Job Creation

Based on detailed state-level data from the May 2006 US Census Bureau Report "Exports from Manufacturing Establishments," IRmep utilizes manufacturing productivity-adjusted input/output tables for 22 categories of manufactured goods to determine direct employment by industry (three-digit standard industry code). IRmep then calculates how many jobs are supported by state and industry for a given export destination utilizing three-digit SIC exports from each state. Indirect upstream and downstream jobs for each direct manufacturing job are estimated per the methodology outlined in "Using Economic Data in Commercial Diplomacy," published by International Commercial Diplomacy Inc. Job opportunity costs are calculated via the export revenues loss multiplier against the best-case benchmark scenario.

Appendix – Best Case US Share of Arab Import Market by Country

(Source: Institute for Research: Middle Eastern Policy, Inc.)

Country	2001	2002	2003	2004	2005
Algeria	10.47%	11.00%	11.50%	12.00%	12.50%
Bahrain	9.62%	9.67%	10.00%	10.50%	11.00%
Comoros	3.06%	4.00%	5.00%	6.00%	7.00%
Djibouti	42.21%	5.00%	6.00%	7.00%	8.00%
Egypt	23.04%	26.00%	27.00%	28.00%	29.00%
Iraq	0.42%	1.38%	5.00%	10.00%	12.00%
Jordan	7.46%	8.88%	9.50%	10.50%	11.50%
Kuwait	12.24%	14.00%	16.00%	18.00%	20.00%
Lebanon	6.33%	7.00%	8.00%	9.00%	10.00%
Libya	0.10%	1.00%	5.00%	10.00%	12.00%
Mauritania	6.42%	7.00%	8.00%	9.00%	10.00%
Morocco	2.31%	4.50%	6.00%	7.00%	8.00%
Oman	5.67%	7.00%	9.00%	11.00%	13.00%
Qatar	9.59%	15.00%	20.00%	25.00%	30.00%
Saudi Arabia	19.64%	25.00%	30.00%	35.00%	40.00%
Somalia	1.93%	2.01%	2.01%	2.01%	2.01%
Sudan	1.09%	1.23%	1.23%	1.23%	1.23%
Syria	5.66%	5.04%	5.04%	5.04%	5.04%
Tunisia	3.12%	3.12%	3.12%	3.12%	3.12%
UAE	9.23%	12.00%	14.00%	16.00%	18.00%
Yemen	6.18%	10.84%	10.84%	10.84%	10.84%

Appendix – Actual US Share of Arab Import Market by Country

(Source: Institute for Research: Middle Eastern Policy, Inc.)

COUNTRY	2001	2002	2003	2004	2005F
Algeria	10.47%	9.29%	3.92%	6.37%	5.15%
Bahrain	9.62%	9.98%	9.92%	5.12%	4.48%
Comoros	3.06%	0.37%	0.63%	0.85%	0.26%
Djibouti	42.21%	21.97%	5.12%	6.50%	4.85%
Egypt	23.04%	18.86%	18.04%	16.16%	13.15%
Iraq	0.42%	0.41%	4.84%	8.65%	7.01%
Jordan	7.46%	9.19%	9.94%	7.26%	7.41%
Kuwait	12.24%	13.90%	15.70%	13.67%	16.14%
Lebanon	6.33%	5.30%	5.18%	5.67%	5.24%
Libya	0.10%	0.29%	0.00%	0.54%	0.77%
Mauritania	6.42%	5.08%	7.75%	15.51%	7.63%
Morocco	2.31%	5.44%	3.65%	3.35%	2.91%
Oman	5.67%	6.48%	5.71%	5.17%	6.81%
Qatar	9.59%	8.05%	7.15%	7.39%	14.70%
Saudi Arabia	19.64%	14.79%	12.46%	13.80%	15.20%
Somalia	1.93%	1.66%	1.75%	2.12%	2.16%
Sudan	1.09%	1.00%	1.10%	1.95%	2.05%
Syria	5.66%	5.59%	4.41%	4.19%	2.63%
Tunisia	3.12%	2.24%	1.66%	2.24%	2.03%
UAE	9.23%	11.68%	9.45%	8.90%	14.09%
Yemen	6.18%	10.17%	6.42%	6.22%	5.19%

Appendix - Arab Student Enrollment in US Higher Education by Country of Origin

(Source: Institute for International Education)

Academic Year	2000-2001	2001-2002	2002-2003	2003-2004	2004-2005
IIE Enrollment	2001	2002	2003	2004	2005
Saudi Arabia	5273	5579	4175	3521	3035
Jordan	2187	2417	2173	1853	1754
Kuwait	3045	2966	2212	1846	1720
Egypt	2255	2409	2155	1822	1574
Lebanon	2005	2435	2364	2179	2040
Morocco	1917	2102	2034	1835	1571
United Arab Emirates	2659	2121	1792	1248	1158
Bahrain	562	601	451	444	377
Tunisia	385	458	381	341	268
Oman	702	623	540	445	354
Syria	713	735	642	556	498
Qatar	463	461	441	354	290
Iraq	155	147	127	120	142
Yemen	411	436	375	284	238
Algeria	220	196	177	148	143
Mauritania	73	79	87	68	58
Sudan	366	378	431	279	290
Comoros	38	44	31	22	23
Djibouti	8	8	5	2	5
Libya	39	42	33	39	39
Somalia	96	87	87	37	55
Palestine	237	232	287	247	66
Total	23809	24556	21000	17690	15698

Appendix - Total Direct US Manufacturing Jobs Generated by Exports to the Arab Market (By Industry)

Jobs Generated	2001	2002	2003	2004	2005
311 Processed Foods	2293	2292	2389	2121	2350
312 Beverage & Tobacco Products	318	198	187	186	167
313 Fabric Mill Products	447	352	261	283	213
314 Non-Apparel Textile Products	168	199	265	265	351
315 Apparel Manufactures	323	257	237	333	315
316 Leather & Related Products	107	99	134	134	123
321 Wood Products	313	325	267	323	289
322 Paper Products	559	535	562	532	609
323 Printing & Related Products	375	546	436	441	452
324 Petroleum & Coal Products	47	100	46	45	57
325 Chemical Manufactures	1867	1464	1530	1920	1917
326 Plastic & Rubber Products	798	827	858	909	971
327 Non-Metallic Mineral Mfgs.	463	447	489	478	618
331 Primary Metal Manufactures	756	862	642	901	1528
332 Fabricated Metal Products	2588	2559	2842	4051	4186
333 Machinery Manufactures	12305	12787	12141	15969	18397
334 Computers & Electronic Prod.	4715	4349	4766	5866	6881
335 Elec. Eq., Appliances & Parts	2651	2507	3255	3507	3683
336 Transportation Equipment	8628	8070	8710	11929	24534
337 Furniture & Related Products	1225	1038	850	920	969
339 Misc. Manufactures	1684	1896	1774	2368	3053
Total	42631	41707	42642	53483	71663

Appendix - Direct US Manufacturing Jobs Generated by Exports to the Arab Market (By Origin of Movement)

	2001	2002	2003	2004	2005
AL	505	605	589	576	701
AK	0	0	0	0	0
AZ	354	291	315	946	376
AR	365	230	167	239	254
CA	2827	2795	2630	3688	6083
CO	117	121	102	160	248
CT	358	299	442	659	569
DE	100	103	75	130	178
DC	0	0	0	0	0
FL	2109	2251	1741	3865	4305
GA	1406	1184	1677	1597	1571
HI	0	0	0	0	0
ID	4	12	19	13	18
IL	1769	1780	2370	2188	2534
IN	600	619	596	780	919
IA	375	355	327	538	471
KS	227	328	184	159	562
KY	218	250	222	213	346
LA	932	1043	857	931	1307
ME	55	77	83	71	45
MD	1315	1216	2234	2058	3043
MA	832	682	917	935	980
MI	2279	2157	2265	2117	2333
MN	370	394	483	529	580
MS	952	222	269	247	2026
MO	668	394	350	367	438
MT	1	1	1	2	2
NE	204	170	177	134	495

NV	30	26	50	38	45
NH	86	121	105	126	197
NJ	1672	1855	1700	2188	2255
NM	15	31	36	45	9
NY	3300	3622	3423	5277	5641
NC	1434	1145	1110	1571	2188
ND	26	19	50	55	43
OH	1444	1992	1956	2551	4546
OK	737	525	791	841	2016
OR	172	192	210	162	226
PA	1118	1046	1261	1376	1512
RI	79	70	44	58	66
SC	526	540	570	637	783
SD	13	15	16	77	115
TN	620	617	558	768	2844
TX	9205	9250	8498	11042	14906
UT	102	83	128	212	285
VT	57	24	32	12	20
VA	1596	1710	1680	1768	1672
WA	428	288	341	419	363
WV	21	42	37	48	96
WI	972	886	929	1034	1414
WY	37	28	31	34	36
Total	42632	41704	42647	53482	71663

Appendix - Direct and Indirect US Jobs Generated by Manufactures Exports to the Arab Market (By Origin of Movement)

	2001	2002	2003	2004	2005
AL	1514	1815	1766	1729	2103
AK	0	0	0	0	0
AZ	1061	873	945	2837	1127
AR	1094	690	502	717	763
CA	8482	8386	7889	11064	18249
CO	350	364	305	480	744
CT	1075	898	1327	1976	1708
DE	299	310	224	391	533
DC	0	0	0	0	0
FL	6327	6752	5223	11596	12916
GA	4218	3552	5030	4792	4714
HI	0	0	0	0	0
ID	12	35	58	40	54
IL	5306	5339	7110	6565	7601
IN	1801	1858	1787	2339	2756
IA	1125	1064	982	1614	1413
KS	681	985	552	476	1685
KY	653	751	665	640	1039
LA	2795	3130	2572	2792	3921
ME	166	230	249	213	136
MD	3944	3647	6703	6174	9128
MA	2497	2046	2752	2805	2941
MI	6836	6470	6796	6352	6999
MN	1111	1181	1449	1588	1741
MS	2855	665	806	742	6077
MO	2004	1183	1051	1102	1315
MT	2	4	3	6	7
NE	611	509	532	401	1486

NV	90	77	150	115	135
NH	257	363	315	379	592
NJ	5016	5564	5099	6563	6764
NM	46	92	107	135	26
NY	9900	10867	10269	15831	16923
NC	4301	3434	3329	4712	6563
ND	77	57	150	165	130
OH	4331	5975	5868	7653	13637
OK	2212	1574	2373	2522	6048
OR	517	577	631	485	677
PA	3355	3138	3782	4129	4535
RI	238	209	131	173	198
SC	1579	1621	1710	1912	2348
SD	40	46	47	231	346
TN	1861	1850	1674	2304	8533
TX	27615	27749	25493	33126	44719
UT	307	249	385	636	855
VT	172	71	96	36	59
VA	4787	5131	5040	5304	5015
WA	1285	864	1024	1257	1090
WV	64	127	112	145	289
WI	2917	2657	2787	3103	4241
WY	111	83	93	101	108
SUM	127897	125111	127940	160446	214988

Appendix - Direct US Manufacturing Jobs Generated by Exports to United Arab Emirates (By Industry)

Industry	2001	2002	2003	2004	2005
311 Processed Foods	367	347	333	335	307
312 Beverage & Tobacco Products	47	34	33	43	46
313 Fabric Mill Products	68	75	66	79	48
314 Non-Apparel Textile Products	45	41	69	69	60
315 Apparel Manufactures	94	101	53	78	97
316 Leather & Related Products	43	40	51	56	58
321 Wood Products	41	48	39	50	52
322 Paper Products	58	81	80	81	106
323 Printing & Related Products	109	95	121	130	147
324 Petroleum & Coal Products	11	12	14	12	14
325 Chemical Manufactures	311	330	335	445	505
326 Plastic & Rubber Products	149	158	172	183	263
327 Non-Metallic Mineral Mfgs.	99	94	113	134	179
331 Primary Metal Manufactures	318	191	174	334	727
332 Fabricated Metal Products	334	460	701	549	620
333 Machinery Manufactures	2842	3653	3205	4043	4468
334 Computers & Electronic Prod.	1161	1171	1324	1618	1748
335 Elec. Eq., Appliances & Parts	411	412	595	690	802
336 Transportation Equipment	778	992	1318	2206	9033
337 Furniture & Related Products	138	146	96	130	221
339 Misc. Manufactures	602	864	744	1165	1704
Total	8026	9344	9635	12429	21205

Appendix - Direct US Manufacturing Jobs Generated by Exports to United Arab Emirates (By Origin of Movement)

State	2001	2002	2003	2004	2005
AL	83	86	115	89	115
AK	0	0	0	0	0
AZ	65	30	78	108	93
AR	53	30	34	36	72
CA	766	872	883	1154	3576
CO	23	23	20	36	45
CT	61	58	168	157	157
DE	8	11	14	12	27
DC	0	0	0	0	0
FL	244	420	524	936	852
GA	212	258	396	402	334
HI	0	0	0	0	0
ID	1	1	0	2	1
IL	373	469	456	465	722
IN	73	66	79	103	118
IA	45	54	72	81	78
KS	34	38	52	47	125
KY	74	84	68	70	90
LA	139	228	117	168	128
ME	19	28	20	21	11
MD	170	167	234	166	174
MA	187	165	185	151	165
MI	142	197	373	381	498
MN	106	127	182	147	156
MS	41	40	43	46	729
MO	90	72	138	91	156
MT	0	0	0	1	1
NE	18	16	29	34	51

NV	6	7	10	12	13
NH	24	28	31	28	29
NJ	278	316	350	403	467
NM	1	3	0	3	2
NY	1129	1229	933	2182	2399
NC	145	148	147	185	250
ND	5	4	6	19	24
OH	297	306	336	610	963
OK	152	188	252	210	297
OR	84	96	90	67	80
PA	201	165	221	273	278
RI	11	12	17	27	30
SC	120	113	163	139	213
SD	2	2	3	21	3
TN	120	121	175	205	978
TX	1911	2443	1947	2435	5801
UT	23	21	15	160	221
VT	24	2	6	3	4
VA	188	315	280	216	220
WA	115	95	164	110	147
WV	4	6	4	9	10
WI	150	177	197	203	295
WY	9	6	8	7	7
Total	8026	9345	9636	12431	21206

Appendix - Direct and Indirect US Jobs Generated by Manufactures Exports to United Arab Emirates (By Origin of Movement)

	2001	2002	2003	2004	2005
AL	250	257	345	266	346
AK	0	0	0	0	0
AZ	195	90	234	324	278
AR	159	90	101	107	215
CA	2297	2616	2649	3462	10727
CO	69	70	61	108	136
CT	184	174	504	471	471
DE	24	34	42	37	82
DC	0	0	0	0	0
FL	733	1261	1572	2808	2556
GA	636	775	1189	1207	1001
HI	0	0	0	0	0
ID	2	2	1	5	3
IL	1119	1407	1369	1395	2166
IN	218	199	236	310	353
IA	135	161	216	243	233
KS	101	113	157	140	374
KY	223	252	203	210	270
LA	418	684	351	503	385
ME	58	83	61	64	32
MD	509	502	701	497	522
MA	560	496	556	454	495
MI	425	590	1120	1144	1495
MN	319	380	545	441	469
MS	123	121	130	139	2187
MO	269	217	413	274	469
MT	1	0	0	2	3
NE	54	49	86	102	153

NV	17	21	29	37	38
NH	72	85	94	85	88
NJ	834	949	1049	1209	1401
NM	4	9	1	9	6
NY	3386	3688	2800	6547	7198
NC	434	444	442	556	751
ND	15	11	18	58	72
OH	891	919	1008	1829	2888
OK	457	563	755	629	891
OR	251	288	271	202	240
PA	603	496	663	818	834
RI	33	35	51	81	90
SC	361	340	488	416	639
SD	5	6	10	62	10
TN	361	362	525	616	2935
TX	5734	7328	5840	7305	17404
UT	69	63	44	480	664
VT	73	5	17	8	12
VA	565	944	841	647	660
WA	344	284	492	331	440
WV	13	19	13	27	30
WI	449	532	591	608	885
WY	26	19	24	21	22
Total	24079	28034	28908	37292	63619

Appendix - Direct US Manufacturing Jobs Generated by Exports to the Saudi Arabian Market (By Industry)

Jobs Generated	2001	2002	2003	2004	2005
311 Processed Foods	735	651	640	593	604
312 Beverage & Tobacco Products	140	87	81	79	51
313 Fabric Mill Products	122	116	98	85	85
314 Non-Apparel Textile Products	81	105	71	44	44
315 Apparel Manufactures	98	73	75	58	69
316 Leather & Related Products	28	32	27	27	27
321 Wood Products	134	133	114	154	120
322 Paper Products	248	220	205	176	179
323 Printing & Related Products	126	114	106	82	110
324 Petroleum & Coal Products	7	5	7	7	8
325 Chemical Manufactures	616	525	574	620	683
326 Plastic & Rubber Products	358	381	365	340	288
327 Non-Metallic Mineral Mfgs.	221	182	174	163	236
331 Primary Metal Manufactures	172	196	147	227	298
332 Fabricated Metal Products	771	700	821	976	802
333 Machinery Manufactures	4335	4046	3713	4969	5456
334 Computers & Electronic Prod.	1350	1391	1365	1234	1373
335 Elec. Eq., Appliances & Parts	1339	1229	1349	1380	1438
336 Transportation Equipment	4234	3928	3135	3885	7362
337 Furniture & Related Products	659	508	364	334	273
339 Misc. Manufactures	550	530	512	503	584
Total	16325	15153	13943	15936	20090

Appendix - Direct US Manufacturing Jobs Generated by Exports to the Saudi Arabian Market (By Origin of Movement)

	2001	2002	2003	2004	2005
AL	182	149	198	184	317
AK	0	0	0	0	0
AZ	138	88	155	46	67
AR	73	156	85	145	125
CA	829	626	647	588	729
CO	54	39	27	48	72
CT	134	109	160	210	167
DE	47	39	25	42	98
DC	0	0	0	0	0
FL	1231	1105	522	1361	1612
GA	533	371	520	399	628
HI	0	0	0	0	0
ID	1	4	1	5	1
IL	712	731	626	672	850
IN	216	234	198	152	190
IA	90	195	112	246	124
KS	87	107	20	37	166
KY	78	101	96	82	152
LA	240	256	214	256	279
ME	8	33	40	21	0
MD	617	506	475	346	421
MA	151	233	301	226	278
MI	1343	1283	943	839	1027
MN	90	115	163	150	203
MS	105	83	72	79	834
MO	177	166	108	87	103
MT	0	1	1	1	0
NE	152	100	84	26	36

NV	5	8	6	7	9
NH	29	32	40	29	29
NJ	852	909	881	1054	1081
NM	5	15	32	38	3
NY	1316	1228	1350	1770	1738
NC	739	494	544	763	606
ND	15	11	27	28	0
OH	652	830	604	841	1301
OK	269	90	168	242	1042
OR	33	37	50	33	46
PA	467	444	381	428	505
RI	37	44	12	13	20
SC	145	163	132	155	142
SD	6	6	5	47	14
TN	202	256	153	272	590
TX	2867	2523	2553	2771	3309
UT	19	26	21	25	23
VT	24	7	3	7	5
VA	799	699	707	724	487
WA	116	80	74	51	70
WV	8	16	11	14	16
WI	405	389	374	346	550
WY	27	19	22	27	22
SUM	16325	15153	13943	15936	20090

Appendix - Direct and Indirect US Jobs Generated by Manufactures Exports to Saudi Arabia (By Origin of Movement)

	2001	2002	2003	2004	2005
AL	546	446	595	551	952
AK	0	0	0	0	0
AZ	413	264	466	138	202
AR	219	469	254	436	376
CA	2486	1877	1940	1763	2186
CO	163	116	82	145	217
CT	402	328	479	630	502
DE	142	118	76	127	294
DC	0	0	0	0	0
FL	3694	3314	1566	4083	4837
GA	1600	1114	1559	1197	1884
HI	0	0	0	0	0
ID	3	12	4	16	4
IL	2137	2194	1878	2015	2549
IN	647	702	595	455	569
IA	270	585	337	737	371
KS	262	321	61	112	499
KY	235	302	287	247	456
LA	719	768	641	767	837
ME	25	99	120	64	0
MD	1850	1518	1424	1039	1262
MA	452	698	902	677	833
MI	4030	3850	2829	2518	3080
MN	269	345	490	451	609
MS	316	249	216	238	2503
MO	532	498	323	262	308
MT	0	3	3	4	1
NE	456	299	251	79	108

NV	15	23	18	22	26
NH	87	97	121	87	88
NJ	2555	2726	2643	3162	3243
NM	15	46	96	113	10
NY	3949	3683	4049	5311	5215
NC	2216	1482	1633	2290	1818
ND	46	32	81	84	0
OH	1957	2489	1812	2524	3903
OK	808	271	504	727	3127
OR	99	110	150	100	139
PA	1400	1331	1143	1284	1515
RI	112	132	35	39	60
SC	434	488	396	465	426
SD	17	18	14	140	41
TN	607	767	459	815	1770
TX	8601	7569	7660	8314	9927
UT	56	78	62	74	69
VT	72	21	10	22	16
VA	2397	2098	2120	2171	1461
WA	349	239	222	153	210
WV	24	49	34	41	48
WI	1215	1168	1123	1039	1650
WY	81	56	67	80	65
SUM	48976	45460	41829	47807	60269

Appendix - Direct US Manufacturing Jobs Generated by Exports to Egypt (By Industry)

Industry	2001	2002	2003	2004	2005
311 Processed Foods	404	424	409	150	333
312 Beverage & Tobacco Products	1	1	3	3	6
313 Fabric Mill Products	13	15	8	16	18
314 Non-Apparel Textile Products	4	5	24	12	13
315 Apparel Manufactures	7	2	2	1	3
316 Leather & Related Products	9	5	4	6	4
321 Wood Products	56	52	42	40	51
322 Paper Products	102	111	115	104	162
323 Printing & Related Products	31	22	16	64	27
324 Petroleum & Coal Products	8	8	9	11	17
325 Chemical Manufactures	571	260	246	371	281
326 Plastic & Rubber Products	78	85	79	112	57
327 Non-Metallic Mineral Mfgs.	42	42	51	58	64
331 Primary Metal Manufactures	96	90	81	81	134
332 Fabricated Metal Products	592	440	463	1376	1183
333 Machinery Manufactures	1578	1500	1457	1655	2073
334 Computers & Electronic Prod.	925	549	505	748	763
335 Elec. Eq., Appliances & Parts	241	208	131	287	265
336 Transportation Equipment	1129	707	1284	1811	1375
337 Furniture & Related Products	42	29	44	42	38
339 Misc. Manufactures	171	118	89	130	132
Total	6102	4673	5062	7076	7000

Appendix - Direct US Manufacturing Jobs Generated by Exports to Egypt (By Origin of Movement)

State	2001	2002	2003	2004	2005
AL	90	109	66	191	29
AK	0	0	0	0	0
AZ	7	15	16	590	5
AR	16	9	6	5	7
CA	288	283	177	579	360
CO	14	15	12	15	24
CT	34	45	30	87	111
DE	12	24	7	28	6
DC	0	0	0	0	0
FL	145	249	118	131	331
GA	196	143	125	127	159
HI	0	0	0	0	0
ID	2	0	0	1	0
IL	215	196	272	201	155
IN	156	68	41	80	63
IA	27	27	62	94	132
KS	61	95	36	17	69
KY	15	23	19	26	23
LA	243	165	198	130	205
ME	20	9	3	5	2
MD	217	149	975	1198	1985
MA	144	48	66	132	59
MI	94	76	174	129	185
MN	86	60	32	51	39
MS	578	28	59	28	25
MO	268	71	18	31	15
MT	0	0	0	0	0
NE	16	12	27	11	26

NV	4	1	30	8	3
NH	7	25	9	15	78
NJ	225	137	118	178	130
NM	1	0	0	0	0
NY	254	278	217	249	473
NC	172	146	73	129	130
ND	2	1	1	1	3
OH	149	185	133	203	177
OK	57	30	115	75	82
OR	19	8	8	12	21
PA	194	156	288	329	133
RI	12	1	1	2	3
SC	114	137	85	82	72
SD	2	1	1	2	3
TN	157	73	54	46	66
TX	1382	1223	1167	1578	1399
UT	28	13	18	5	7
VT	1	1	1	0	1
VA	139	214	110	101	87
WA	69	26	21	20	22
WV	4	9	2	3	3
WI	166	85	68	147	87
WY	0	1	0	0	0
Total	6102	4668	5059	7074	6998

Appendix - Direct and Indirect US Jobs Generated by Manufactures Exports to Egypt (By Origin of Movement)

State	2001	2002	2003	2004	2005
AL	270	327	198	572	88
AK	0	0	0	0	0
AZ	20	44	49	1771	16
AR	48	26	19	16	20
CA	865	849	530	1737	1080
CO	43	44	37	46	73
CT	101	135	91	262	332
DE	37	73	20	83	18
DC	0	0	0	0	0
FL	435	747	355	392	992
GA	588	428	375	382	478
HI	0	0	0	0	0
ID	6	0	1	2	0
IL	644	588	815	604	464
IN	468	203	123	240	189
IA	81	82	186	281	396
KS	184	285	109	50	208
KY	46	68	58	77	70
LA	729	496	593	391	614
ME	60	26	10	16	7
MD	650	448	2926	3593	5955
MA	431	144	199	396	177
MI	283	227	521	388	554
MN	258	181	95	153	118
MS	1735	84	178	84	76
MO	804	214	55	94	45
MT	0	0	0	0	1
NE	49	37	82	33	77

NV	13	3	89	23	9
NH	20	75	27	45	234
NJ	676	411	354	534	391
NM	2	0	0	1	1
NY	761	835	650	748	1419
NC	517	437	219	388	391
ND	5	3	2	3	10
OH	448	556	399	609	530
OK	170	89	344	224	246
OR	58	25	23	37	63
PA	581	467	863	987	400
RI	35	2	3	5	8
SC	341	411	255	246	217
SD	7	2	3	5	8
TN	471	219	163	138	198
TX	4145	3668	3500	4735	4196
UT	85	40	54	15	22
VT	2	2	4	1	4
VA	418	641	329	303	261
WA	208	77	62	60	66
WV	12	26	7	9	10
WI	497	256	203	442	260
WY	0	4	0	0	0
TOTAL	18305	14005	15177	21221	20993

Appendix - Direct US Manufacturing Jobs
Generated by Exports to Kuwait (By Industry)

Jobs Generated	2001	2002	2003	2004	2005
311 Processed Foods	137	141	338	189	200
312 Beverage & Tobacco Products	25	13	16	13	11
313 Fabric Mill Products	17	9	15	35	9
314 Non-Apparel Textile Products	6	13	46	69	134
315 Apparel Manufactures	49	37	57	63	51
316 Leather & Related Products	11	6	12	11	11
321 Wood Products	11	12	9	12	8
322 Paper Products	16	13	18	12	12
323 Printing & Related Products	31	30	49	43	40
324 Petroleum & Coal Products	1	1	1	2	2
325 Chemical Manufactures	79	87	98	125	119
326 Plastic & Rubber Products	75	72	86	125	117
327 Non-Metallic Mineral Mfgs.	23	25	27	28	42
331 Primary Metal Manufactures	17	136	102	91	121
332 Fabricated Metal Products	294	207	366	241	306
333 Machinery Manufactures	680	845	874	1075	1065
334 Computers & Electronic Prod.	226	220	573	470	481
335 Elec. Eq., Appliances & Parts	164	137	304	285	251
336 Transportation Equipment	1008	1343	1679	1772	2910
337 Furniture & Related Products	199	187	187	177	182
339 Misc. Manufactures	90	95	141	154	169
Total	3161	3629	4998	4993	6244

Appendix - Direct US Manufacturing Jobs Generated by Exports to Kuwait (By Origin of Movement)

State	2001	2002	2003	2004	2005
AL	33	132	103	46	110
AK	0	0	0	0	0
AZ	0	0	0	0	0
AR	8	6	9	9	15
CA	249	253	248	376	301
CO	7	8	13	12	23
CT	27	19	30	39	17
DE	4	3	12	14	12
DC	0	0	0	0	0
FL	204	220	265	559	411
GA	104	123	114	111	87
HI	0	0	0	0	0
ID	0	0	1	0	0
IL	63	102	251	177	172
IN	48	28	156	103	49
IA	152	26	19	31	42
KS	8	24	12	13	39
KY	9	6	15	9	9
LA	22	25	49	24	15
ME	2	1	7	7	13
MD	57	97	171	101	117
MA	61	48	168	88	57
MI	479	412	525	528	333
MN	19	16	24	50	34
MS	27	33	38	29	122
MO	66	40	32	86	64
MT	0	0	0	0	0
NE	2	2	5	8	19

NV	1	1	2	3	2
NH	1	6	11	5	7
NJ	109	114	158	155	155
NM	0	0	0	2	0
NY	128	140	176	203	204
NC	120	115	135	189	201
ND	0	1	5	2	4
OH	143	420	608	321	1092
OK	51	74	80	90	283
OR	7	9	16	24	14
PA	66	71	100	115	157
RI	5	5	4	8	5
SC	44	44	76	76	62
SD	1	1	2	4	15
TN	48	57	58	80	628
TX	530	665	880	869	1028
UT	3	10	43	3	7
VT	2	1	0	0	1
VA	158	182	247	225	138
WA	13	22	22	46	22
WV	2	8	11	18	50
WI	74	57	97	135	105
WY	0	0	0	0	0
Total	3161	3629	4998	4993	6244

Appendix - Direct and Indirect US Jobs Generated by Manufactures Exports to Kuwait (By Origin of Movement)

	2001	2002	2003	2004	2005
AL	99	395	308	138	330
AK	0	0	0	0	0
AZ	0	0	0	0	0
AR	25	19	27	28	46
CA	748	758	743	1129	902
CO	22	24	39	35	69
CT	81	57	90	116	51
DE	11	10	36	42	35
DC	0	0	0	0	0
FL	612	659	795	1676	1234
GA	311	369	341	332	261
HI	0	0	0	0	0
ID	0	0	4	1	1
IL	188	307	754	531	516
IN	145	83	469	309	147
IA	457	79	58	94	127
KS	24	71	36	38	117
KY	28	18	45	26	26
LA	66	75	147	71	46
ME	5	2	21	21	40
MD	172	290	513	303	351
MA	183	144	504	264	171
MI	1437	1235	1576	1584	1000
MN	57	47	72	151	103
MS	80	99	114	88	366
MO	198	121	97	257	193
MT	1	0	0	1	1
NE	7	5	15	24	57

NV	3	18	33	15	20
NH	3	3	5	8	5
NJ	327	342	475	466	466
NM	0	0	0	5	1
NY	383	421	527	608	611
NC	360	345	405	566	604
ND	0	2	14	5	13
OH	430	1261	1825	964	3275
OK	154	223	240	270	848
OR	22	28	48	72	43
PA	199	212	299	346	472
RI	14	16	11	24	14
SC	133	132	227	227	186
SD	3	3	6	12	45
TN	145	172	175	239	1883
TX	1589	1994	2639	2606	3085
UT	10	30	128	9	22
VT	6	4	1	1	4
VA	474	547	741	676	414
WA	40	67	66	139	67
WV	7	24	34	55	149
WI	221	172	291	406	316
WY	0	0	0	0	0
TOTAL	9482	10887	14994	14978	18731

Appendix - Direct US Manufacturing Jobs
Generated by Exports to Iraq (By Industry)

Jobs Generated	2001	2002	2003	2004	2005
311 Processed Foods	0	0	114	56	202
312 Beverage & Tobacco Products	0	0	0	0	0
313 Fabric Mill Products	0	0	0	1	1
314 Non-Apparel Textile Products	0	0	1	25	31
315 Apparel Manufactures	0	0	6	75	35
316 Leather & Related Products	0	0	2	7	4
321 Wood Products	0	0	0	0	1
322 Paper Products	0	0	0	3	2
323 Printing & Related Products	0	0	10	5	5
324 Petroleum & Coal Products	0	0	0	0	0
325 Chemical Manufactures	0	0	5	12	5
326 Plastic & Rubber Products	0	0	21	20	36
327 Non-Metallic Mineral Mfgs.	1	0	0	7	8
331 Primary Metal Manufactures	1	0	2	21	6
332 Fabricated Metal Products	5	0	6	163	85
333 Machinery Manufactures	120	141	345	1005	830
334 Computers & Electronic Prod.	22	3	42	679	1388
335 Elec. Eq., Appliances & Parts	17	1	472	253	86
336 Transportation Equipment	7	3	55	488	819
337 Furniture & Related Products	0	0	0	42	11
339 Misc. Manufactures	1	0	3	74	112
Total	173	149	1084	2934	3668

Appendix - Direct US Manufacturing Jobs Generated by Exports to Iraq (By Origin of Movement)

	2001	2002	2003	2004	2005
AL	0	0	15	32	33
AK	0	0	0	0	0
AZ	0	0	0	40	131
AR	0	0	4	6	5
CA	0	2	6	95	114
CO	0	0	3	14	26
CT	0	0	10	11	10
DE	0	0	0	0	0
DC	0	0	0	0	0
FL	0	0	39	203	396
GA	0	0	156	233	81
HI	0	0	0	0	0
ID	0	0	8	1	1
IL	91	4	426	150	178
IN	0	0	4	35	14
IA	0	0	1	3	14
KS	0	0	2	3	8
KY	0	0	0	3	22
LA	0	0	26	0	328
ME	0	0	0	2	2
MD	0	0	10	47	104
MA	0	0	2	158	192
MI	1	0	1	17	20
MN	0	0	1	12	7
MS	0	0	0	18	0
MO	0	0	3	4	17
MT	0	0	0	0	0
NE	0	14	0	2	7
NV	0	0	0	0	6

NH	0	0	0	21	28
NJ	0	0	23	74	28
NM	0	0	0	0	0
NY	0	0	196	62	130
NC	0	0	10	78	671
ND	0	0	0	0	0
OH	0	0	4	193	49
OK	0	0	17	48	5
OR	0	0	1	4	9
PA	2	8	7	64	138
RI	0	0	0	1	1
SC	0	1	4	46	171
SD	0	0	0	0	71
TN	0	0	17	25	34
TX	27	110	77	1017	360
UT	17	0	0	8	12
VT	0	0	0	0	0
VA	4	0	11	128	210
WA	30	7	2	67	20
WV	0	0	0	1	9
WI	0	1	5	8	8
WY	0	0	0	0	0
TOTAL	173	149	1093	2935	3669

Appendix - Direct and Indirect US Jobs Generated by Manufactures Exports to Iraq (By Origin of Movement)

	2001	2002	2003	2004	2005
AL	0	0	44	95	99
AK	0	0	0	0	0
AZ	0	0	1	121	393
AR	0	0	12	17	14
CA	0	5	19	286	343
CO	0	0	9	43	78
CT	0	0	29	32	31
DE	0	0	0	1	1
DC	0	0	0	0	0
FL	0	0	118	610	1188
GA	0	0	467	699	243
HI	0	0	0	0	0
ID	0	0	25	2	3
IL	274	13	1279	451	535
IN	0	0	13	104	41
IA	0	0	4	9	43
KS	0	0	7	9	23
KY	0	0	1	8	65
LA	0	0	78	1	985
ME	0	0	0	5	5
MD	0	0	30	140	311
MA	0	1	7	474	575
MI	3	1	2	52	61
MN	0	0	4	36	22
MS	0	0	0	53	1
MO	0	0	10	11	52
MT	0	0	0	0	0
NE	0	42	0	5	22

NV	0	0	0	1	18
NH	0	0	0	63	84
NJ	0	0	69	221	83
NM	0	0	0	1	0
NY	0	0	587	187	389
NC	0	0	29	235	2013
ND	0	0	0	0	1
OH	0	0	11	578	147
OK	0	0	50	145	14
OR	0	0	2	13	28
PA	6	25	21	193	413
RI	0	0	0	2	3
SC	0	2	11	137	514
SD	0	0	0	0	212
TN	0	0	51	76	101
TX	80	331	231	3052	1081
UT	51	0	0	24	35
VT	0	0	0	0	0
VA	13	0	33	383	629
WA	91	22	7	201	61
WV	0	0	0	2	28
WI	0	3	16	25	23
WY	0	0	0	0	0
TOTAL	519	447	3278	8805	11007

Appendix - Direct US Manufacturing Jobs Generated by Exports to Algeria (By Industry)

Jobs Generated	2001	2002	2003	2004	2005
311 Processed Foods	144	149	91	151	84
312 Beverage & Tobacco Products	0	0	0	0	0
313 Fabric Mill Products	9	1	12	12	1
314 Non-Apparel Textile Products	2	1	12	2	1
315 Apparel Manufactures	0	1	0	2	1
316 Leather & Related Products	1	0	0	1	0
321 Wood Products	4	0	1	1	1
322 Paper Products	15	6	8	12	16
323 Printing & Related Products	1	1	1	5	0
324 Petroleum & Coal Products	4	0	0	0	0
325 Chemical Manufactures	12	35	33	63	39
326 Plastic & Rubber Products	19	21	8	16	52
327 Non-Metallic Mineral Mfgs.	19	18	20	11	14
331 Primary Metal Manufactures	42	135	41	32	83
332 Fabricated Metal Products	129	114	43	148	140
333 Machinery Manufactures	777	577	528	1010	951
334 Computers & Electronic Prod.	134	222	82	173	164
335 Elec. Eq., Appliances & Parts	42	63	16	93	103
336 Transportation Equipment	150	111	64	145	134
337 Furniture & Related Products	0	1	0	0	0
339 Misc. Manufactures	1	7	3	16	7
Total	1507	1462	963	1892	1790

Appendix - Direct US Manufacturing Jobs Generated by Exports to Algeria (By Origin of Movement)

	2001	2002	2003	2004	2005
AL	12	15	4	0	0
AK	0	0	0	0	0
AZ	2	1	2	63	11
AR	1	0	2	0	1
CA	32	42	32	60	133
CO	0	3	7	5	12
CT	35	14	2	7	2
DE	3	0	0	0	0
DC	0	0	0	0	0
FL	49	47	29	89	76
GA	116	12	49	49	76
HI	0	0	0	0	0
ID	0	5	6	4	9
IL	65	41	21	59	52
IN	1	2	4	5	7
IA	25	3	18	4	26
KS	3	8	0	2	19
KY	1	1	0	1	9
LA	132	137	76	129	63
ME	0	0	0	1	0
MD	0	0	0	1	0
MA	10	4	14	6	31
MI	3	0	1	1	9
MN	4	6	14	25	4
MS	14	5	24	10	1
MO	0	2	3	2	4
MT	0	0	0	0	0
NE	2	3	0	2	16
NV	0	0	0	1	3

NH	0	0	1	1	0
NJ	14	4	16	15	9
NM	0	0	0	0	0
NY	39	156	38	359	46
NC	7	4	3	5	48
ND	1	0	1	1	6
OH	9	3	9	7	21
OK	37	15	10	31	23
OR	0	0	0	1	14
PA	7	11	6	25	48
RI	0	0	0	0	0
SC	2	3	6	22	8
SD	0	0	0	0	2
TN	1	5	1	8	32
TX	871	884	537	828	874
UT	0	1	0	0	1
VT	0	3	2	0	0
VA	7	6	17	46	79
WA	3	6	2	13	15
WV	0	0	1	0	0
WI	0	11	4	3	0
WY	0	0	0	0	0
TOTAL	1507	1462	963	1892	1790

Appendix - Direct and Indirect US Jobs Generated by Manufactures Exports to Algeria (By Origin of Movement)

	2001	2002	2003	2004	2005
AL	36	45	13	0	1
AK	0	0	0	0	0
AZ	6	3	6	188	33
AR	4	0	6	1	2
CA	96	125	95	181	398
CO	0	8	21	16	36
CT	105	41	6	20	6
DE	10	1	0	0	0
DC	0	0	0	0	0
FL	146	140	88	268	228
GA	347	36	147	148	229
HI	0	0	0	0	0
ID	1	16	18	13	26
IL	196	122	63	176	157
IN	2	6	12	16	22
IA	75	8	55	13	79
KS	9	25	1	5	58
KY	2	3	1	4	27
LA	395	410	227	388	189
ME	0	0	0	4	0
MD	0	0	0	3	0
MA	31	11	41	19	92
MI	10	0	3	4	26
MN	11	19	41	76	11
MS	43	14	72	30	2
MO	0	6	9	6	12
MT	0	0	0	0	0
NE	5	9	1	5	47
NV	0	0	1	4	9

NH	0	0	2	4	1
NJ	42	11	49	46	27
NM	0	0	0	0	0
NY	116	469	113	1077	138
NC	21	11	9	14	143
ND	2	1	4	3	18
OH	26	8	27	20	62
OK	112	46	29	92	69
OR	0	1	0	2	42
PA	21	34	17	74	144
RI	1	0	0	0	0
SC	6	8	19	66	24
SD	0	0	0	1	7
TN	3	15	4	23	97
TX	2613	2653	1612	2483	2623
UT	0	2	0	0	3
VT	0	9	6	0	0
VA	20	19	51	137	237
WA	8	17	6	38	45
WV	0	0	2	0	0
WI	0	33	12	8	0
WY	0	0	0	0	0
TOTAL	4521	4386	2889	5677	5370

Appendix - Direct US Manufacturing Jobs Generated by Exports to Qatar (By Industry)

Jobs Generated	2001	2002	2003	2004	2005
311 Processed Foods	27	45	35	27	36
312 Beverage & Tobacco Products	4	3	4	4	4
313 Fabric Mill Products	2	2	1	8	5
314 Non-Apparel Textile Products	4	2	10	12	11
315 Apparel Manufactures	8	5	6	8	8
316 Leather & Related Products	1	1	3	5	3
321 Wood Products	9	7	7	7	10
322 Paper Products	2	2	1	2	3
323 Printing & Related Products	9	6	8	10	21
324 Petroleum & Coal Products	0	0	0	0	0
325 Chemical Manufactures	50	21	29	23	47
326 Plastic & Rubber Products	10	12	10	19	22
327 Non-Metallic Mineral Mfgs.	8	14	26	26	31
331 Primary Metal Manufactures	14	7	14	24	36
332 Fabricated Metal Products	123	54	87	102	334
333 Machinery Manufactures	414	403	596	588	1618
334 Computers & Electronic Prod.	189	130	168	214	181
335 Elec. Eq., Appliances & Parts	34	46	46	74	133
336 Transportation Equipment	281	216	311	375	900
337 Furniture & Related Products	30	38	44	41	129
339 Misc. Manufactures	42	33	56	45	50
Total	1260	1048	1460	1614	3582

Appendix - Direct US Manufacturing Jobs Generated by Exports to Qatar (By Origin of Movement)

	2001	2002	2003	2004	2005
AL	6	8	9	5	35
AK	0	0	0	0	0
AZ	4	9	20	12	13
AR	4	11	3	2	5
CA	83	111	94	120	156
CO	1	16	4	4	14
CT	5	8	5	76	20
DE	7	4	4	7	5
DC	0	0	0	0	0
FL	37	14	22	157	188
GA	39	54	80	100	57
HI	0	0	0	0	0
ID	0	0	1	0	0
IL	37	37	51	107	111
IN	7	19	25	14	13
IA	4	4	5	8	18
KS	4	4	8	10	53
KY	4	3	6	2	15
LA	16	5	6	3	15
ME	1	0	4	5	5
MD	9	15	32	15	29
MA	83	22	24	18	26
MI	38	46	48	52	74
MN	9	5	10	13	15
MS	143	5	5	4	83
MO	5	4	8	11	18
MT	0	0	0	0	0
NE	1	1	22	40	302
NV	3	1	1	3	7

NH	1	1	1	6	6
NJ	27	30	21	75	68
NM	0	0	0	0	0
NY	52	113	186	64	214
NC	14	32	23	27	74
ND	0	0	3	0	2
OH	15	69	52	55	546
OK	12	6	16	30	83
OR	3	7	2	2	15
PA	22	27	142	26	130
RI	1	2	3	1	1
SC	12	10	14	9	20
SD	0	3	3	3	4
TN	9	10	10	22	177
TX	494	262	292	429	649
UT	1	2	6	3	5
VT	0	5	18	0	7
VA	19	35	111	43	86
WA	5	12	22	7	25
WV	0	1	5	1	4
WI	23	16	32	20	181
WY	0	0	0	0	7
TOTAL	1260	1048	1460	1614	3582

Appendix - Direct and Indirect US Jobs Generated by Manufactures Exports to Qatar (By Origin of Movement)

	2001	2002	2003	2004	2005
AL	19	25	27	16	105
AK	0	0	0	0	0
AZ	11	28	59	36	39
AR	12	33	10	7	14
CA	250	333	282	361	469
CO	3	49	12	12	41
CT	15	23	14	229	61
DE	21	12	11	22	15
DC	0	0	0	0	0
FL	112	42	65	472	564
GA	116	161	240	301	170
HI	0	0	0	0	0
ID	0	0	4	0	1
IL	111	112	152	322	332
IN	20	56	75	43	40
IA	13	11	14	23	54
KS	12	12	24	29	160
KY	13	9	19	6	46
LA	47	16	18	10	46
ME	2	1	13	15	16
MD	28	45	97	44	88
MA	248	66	71	54	79
MI	115	137	145	155	223
MN	26	16	30	40	46
MS	430	16	14	12	250
MO	14	11	23	32	53
MT	0	0	0	0	0
NE	2	3	66	120	906
NV	8	4	3	9	21

NH	3	3	2	18	17
NJ	80	89	63	225	203
NM	0	1	1	0	1
NY	156	339	559	192	641
NC	43	96	68	81	223
ND	1	1	10	1	6
OH	45	206	157	165	1637
OK	37	19	49	90	250
OR	10	20	7	6	44
PA	66	80	426	78	389
RI	3	6	9	3	4
SC	35	31	42	28	60
SD	0	8	9	8	11
TN	26	31	30	65	531
TX	1482	786	876	1288	1946
UT	3	6	19	8	15
VT	1	16	53	1	21
VA	58	104	333	129	257
WA	15	36	67	20	76
WV	1	2	16	2	11
WI	68	47	96	60	544
WY	0	0	0	0	21
TOTAL	3781	3143	4381	4841	10745

Appendix - Direct US Manufacturing Jobs Generated by Exports to Jordan (By Industry)

Jobs Generated	2001	2002	2003	2004	2005
311 Processed Foods	76	90	96	120	159
312 Beverage & Tobacco Products	19	13	1	1	1
313 Fabric Mill Products	10	28	4	5	6
314 Non-Apparel Textile Products	2	10	6	6	18
315 Apparel Manufactures	4	4	5	7	4
316 Leather & Related Products	2	3	7	3	3
321 Wood Products	10	9	8	11	9
322 Paper Products	27	25	24	28	23
323 Printing & Related Products	8	19	14	29	16
324 Petroleum & Coal Products	0	0	0	0	0
325 Chemical Manufactures	29	35	33	51	49
326 Plastic & Rubber Products	18	18	36	17	33
327 Non-Metallic Mineral Mfgs.	6	5	4	5	6
331 Primary Metal Manufactures	12	45	20	43	67
332 Fabricated Metal Products	40	156	86	233	430
333 Machinery Manufactures	120	126	144	236	347
334 Computers & Electronic Prod.	135	210	253	214	248
335 Elec. Eq., Appliances & Parts	36	56	33	57	62
336 Transportation Equipment	111	200	259	245	383
337 Furniture & Related Products	38	40	42	83	44
339 Misc. Manufactures	58	96	49	79	78
Total	763	1187	1122	1472	1988

Appendix - Direct US Manufacturing Jobs Generated by Exports to Jordan (By Origin of Movement)

State	2001	2002	2003	2004	2005
AL	12	26	29	9	31
AK	0	0	0	0	0
AZ	3	3	5	27	13
AR	0	4	3	8	4
CA	105	163	86	141	199
CO	4	4	2	3	7
CT	6	14	6	36	49
DE	4	2	3	10	9
DC	0	0	0	0	0
FL	23	56	65	110	117
GA	23	49	54	34	25
HI	0	0	0	0	0
ID	0	0	0	0	5
IL	25	34	109	131	81
IN	35	134	7	184	354
IA	1	26	10	33	10
KS	2	2	16	7	35
KY	16	13	7	10	11
LA	22	33	43	22	18
ME	3	1	1	2	3
MD	17	16	176	84	64
MA	31	48	54	34	53
MI	11	13	53	37	44
MN	7	18	14	16	25
MS	7	4	5	10	5
MO	6	5	4	7	13
MT	0	0	0	0	0
NE	2	10	2	3	7
NV	0	0	0	1	1

NH	3	5	1	1	2
NJ	25	36	37	69	83
NM	8	12	2	2	1
NY	99	114	41	56	85
NC	47	46	29	38	54
ND	0	0	5	1	0
OH	21	30	34	52	80
OK	2	2	2	7	8
OR	3	14	4	5	2
PA	23	32	13	29	33
RI	10	2	5	3	3
SC	12	4	16	24	13
SD	1	0	0	1	3
TN	10	25	13	32	51
TX	56	136	87	110	163
UT	6	2	13	1	2
VT	3	3	0	0	0
VA	29	22	50	50	190
WA	24	9	6	9	6
WV	1	1	0	0	0
WI	17	14	10	22	22
WY	0	1	0	0	0
TOTAL	763	1187	1121	1472	1988

Appendix - Direct and Indirect US Jobs Generated by Manufactures Exports to Jordan (By Origin of Movement)

State	2001	2002	2003	2004	2005
AL	35	77	87	27	94
AK	0	0	0	0	0
AZ	10	8	14	82	40
AR	1	11	8	25	11
CA	316	488	259	424	598
CO	13	12	5	9	22
CT	18	42	19	108	147
DE	11	7	9	30	26
DC	0	0	0	0	0
FL	68	167	194	329	352
GA	69	148	163	101	76
HI	0	0	0	0	0
ID	1	0	0	1	16
IL	76	103	327	394	243
IN	104	401	22	551	1062
IA	4	79	31	99	31
KS	5	5	47	20	106
KY	47	38	20	30	33
LA	66	100	129	65	54
ME	8	4	3	6	8
MD	50	47	527	252	193
MA	93	145	162	101	159
MI	34	40	160	112	133
MN	20	53	43	48	76
MS	20	12	16	30	16
MO	19	15	11	22	39
MT	0	0	0	0	0
NE	6	29	6	8	22
NV	0	1	0	3	2

NH	9	16	3	4	5
NJ	76	107	111	208	249
NM	23	35	7	6	4
NY	298	343	122	169	255
NC	141	137	88	114	161
ND	0	1	15	3	1
OH	62	90	102	155	241
OK	7	6	6	20	25
OR	8	41	12	15	6
PA	69	95	38	88	99
RI	29	7	14	8	8
SC	35	13	47	71	39
SD	4	1	1	2	10
TN	31	75	38	96	152
TX	168	407	261	331	488
UT	17	7	39	4	7
VT	9	8	0	1	1
VA	86	67	149	150	571
WA	71	28	18	26	17
WV	3	2	1	1	1
WI	51	42	31	66	65
WY	1	3	0	0	0
TOTAL	2289	3562	3364	4415	5963

Appendix - Direct US Manufacturing Jobs Generated by Exports to Oman (By Industry)

Jobs Generated	2001	2002	2003	2004	2005
311 Processed Foods	47	41	35	43	27
312 Beverage & Tobacco Products	5	3	4	3	3
313 Fabric Mill Products	1	2	2	2	2
314 Non-Apparel Textile Products	6	3	1	2	3
315 Apparel Manufactures	1	0	2	1	1
316 Leather & Related Products	1	1	1	1	1
321 Wood Products	2	2	4	4	1
322 Paper Products	3	4	5	6	6
323 Printing & Related Products	4	3	2	2	2
324 Petroleum & Coal Products	1	0	0	0	0
325 Chemical Manufactures	28	25	29	32	42
326 Plastic & Rubber Products	28	15	19	24	25
327 Non-Metallic Mineral Mfgs.	11	28	25	16	3
331 Primary Metal Manufactures	4	9	4	9	10
332 Fabricated Metal Products	29	25	61	90	72
333 Machinery Manufactures	401	318	391	419	438
334 Computers & Electronic Prod.	105	82	93	92	77
335 Elec. Eq., Appliances & Parts	44	43	30	22	60
336 Transportation Equipment	133	103	122	186	749
337 Furniture & Related Products	8	5	4	4	6
339 Misc. Manufactures	16	18	17	20	22
Total	879	730	849	979	1548

Appendix - Direct US Jobs Generated by Manufactures Exports to Oman (By Origin of Movement)

	2001	2002	2003	2004	2005
AL	7	11	2	3	6
AK	0	0	0	0	0
AZ	9	6	24	1	4
AR	6	2	2	4	1
CA	60	59	97	54	69
CO	3	4	6	10	6
CT	8	9	7	7	10
DE	1	1	2	5	6
DC	0	0	0	0	0
FL	30	16	15	91	59
GA	42	37	37	26	29
HI	0	0	0	0	0
ID	0	0	0	0	0
IL	29	25	35	32	53
IN	9	5	2	5	6
IA	5	3	9	19	7
KS	2	6	3	2	2
KY	5	4	1	1	2
LA	7	11	9	9	8
ME	1	0	0	1	0
MD	27	26	32	22	62
MA	29	29	27	21	18
MI	50	46	36	29	33
MN	4	5	11	8	9
MS	2	2	3	3	191
MO	10	5	5	3	7
MT	0	0	0	0	0
NE	0	1	2	1	0

NV	1	1	0	1	1
NH	1	0	0	0	3
NJ	9	12	8	9	17
NM	0	0	0	0	0
NY	37	27	24	28	28
NC	5	10	7	7	8
ND	1	0	0	0	0
OH	39	22	21	39	86
OK	84	26	39	38	39
OR	5	2	4	2	2
PA	9	10	17	22	15
RI	1	0	1	1	1
SC	13	5	8	6	11
SD	0	0	1	0	0
TN	12	9	6	11	146
TX	283	257	321	378	565
UT	0	4	0	4	2
VT	0	0	0	0	0
VA	15	13	12	58	10
WA	4	2	2	1	2
WV	0	0	0	0	0
WI	15	14	10	18	22
WY	1	0	1	0	0
TOTAL	879	729	849	979	1548

Appendix - Direct and Indirect US Jobs Generated by Manufactures Exports to Oman (By Origin of Movement)

	2001	2002	2003	2004	2005
AL	20	34	5	8	18
AK	0	0	0	0	0
AZ	26	18	73	4	11
AR	18	6	5	11	4
CA	180	177	290	162	208
CO	10	12	18	29	18
CT	25	27	22	21	30
DE	3	3	6	16	19
DC	0	0	0	0	0
FL	89	47	44	273	178
GA	126	112	110	78	86
HI	0	0	0	0	0
ID	0	0	0	0	0
IL	87	74	106	95	159
IN	26	14	7	15	17
IA	14	10	27	58	21
KS	7	18	8	7	6
KY	14	13	4	3	5
LA	20	33	28	27	23
ME	2	1	1	3	1
MD	81	79	96	65	186
MA	88	87	80	62	54
MI	151	137	107	87	100
MN	13	14	34	25	26
MS	7	7	9	8	572
MO	30	14	14	10	20
MT	0	0	0	0	0
NE	1	2	6	3	1
NV	3	2	1	3	2

NH	2	1	0	1	8
NJ	27	36	23	27	52
NM	0	0	0	0	0
NY	110	81	72	84	85
NC	14	30	21	20	24
ND	2	0	0	0	1
OH	116	67	62	116	259
OK	253	79	118	115	118
OR	14	6	11	5	7
PA	26	30	50	65	45
RI	2	1	2	2	2
SC	40	15	25	17	32
SD	0	0	3	0	1
TN	35	28	19	32	438
TX	848	770	963	1135	1696
UT	1	11	1	11	5
VT	1	0	0	0	0
VA	46	38	37	173	30
WA	12	6	7	3	7
WV	1	1	1	0	1
WI	45	43	29	53	67
WY	2	1	2	0	0
TOTAL	2638	2187	2548	2936	4645

Appendix - Direct US Manufacturing Jobs Generated by Exports to Morocco (By Industry)

Jobs Generated	2001	2002	2003	2004	2005
311 Processed Foods	25	74	27	31	35
312 Beverage & Tobacco Products	0	0	3	5	5
313 Fabric Mill Products	77	38	13	9	8
314 Non-Apparel Textile Products	1	6	2	2	1
315 Apparel Manufactures	27	6	4	5	2
316 Leather & Related Products	0	1	1	2	2
321 Wood Products	4	3	2	2	3
322 Paper Products	23	16	22	13	17
323 Printing & Related Products	2	4	5	4	3
324 Petroleum & Coal Products	6	3	3	2	3
325 Chemical Manufactures	39	30	33	37	39
326 Plastic & Rubber Products	10	15	14	13	11
327 Non-Metallic Mineral Mfgs.	4	18	21	11	5
331 Primary Metal Manufactures	14	14	31	6	11
332 Fabricated Metal Products	40	48	37	36	31
333 Machinery Manufactures	112	123	134	180	148
334 Computers & Electronic Prod.	99	76	67	92	93
335 Elec. Eq., Appliances & Parts	45	31	15	55	89
336 Transportation Equipment	40	58	78	80	85
337 Furniture & Related Products	26	9	9	8	12
339 Misc. Manufactures	17	13	25	17	28
Total	609	587	544	607	631

Appendix - Direct US Manufacturing Jobs Generated by Exports to Morocco (By Origin of Movement)

	2001	2002	2003	2004	2005
AL	14	3	8	1	2
AK	0	0	0	0	0
AZ	1	3	5	2	3
AR	1	1	2	2	3
CA	85	89	75	72	74
CO	2	2	1	3	3
CT	31	6	3	8	6
DE	0	1	0	1	1
DC	0	0	0	0	0
FL	31	25	30	24	21
GA	30	23	24	23	19
HI	0	0	0	0	0
ID	0	0	0	0	0
IL	32	40	14	49	23
IN	18	6	8	14	23
IA	7	1	4	2	5
KS	1	8	16	1	15
KY	0	0	0	1	3
LA	15	52	22	6	6
ME	0	1	2	3	2
MD	10	28	25	13	28
MA	17	12	8	15	19
MI	5	10	14	12	7
MN	16	15	11	17	32
MS	3	2	4	4	3
MO	10	8	6	13	14
MT	0	0	0	0	0
NE	0	0	0	0	0
NV	0	0	0	0	0

NH	3	0	2	4	2
NJ	31	30	20	22	13
NM	0	0	0	0	0
NY	34	57	56	78	63
NC	32	20	18	43	19
ND	0	0	0	1	0
OH	28	11	18	19	39
OK	0	2	5	2	57
OR	13	8	23	4	1
PA	6	10	27	10	7
RI	0	0	0	0	0
SC	10	12	15	10	13
SD	0	0	0	0	0
TN	9	7	6	13	4
TX	56	51	23	42	21
UT	0	0	0	0	0
VT	0	0	0	0	0
VA	31	29	35	42	31
WA	11	4	1	13	6
WV	0	0	0	0	2
WI	16	12	13	19	43
WY	0	0	0	0	0
TOTAL	609	587	544	607	631

Appendix - Direct and Indirect US Jobs Generated by Manufactures Exports to Morocco (By Origin of Movement)

	2001	2002	2003	2004	2005
AL	43	8	24	4	6
AK	0	0	0	0	0
AZ	2	10	16	6	10
AR	4	2	5	6	10
CA	255	266	224	215	222
CO	7	7	3	9	9
CT	92	17	10	25	17
DE	0	4	1	2	3
DC	0	0	0	0	0
FL	93	76	90	73	62
GA	90	68	72	68	56
HI	0	0	0	0	0
ID	0	0	0	0	0
IL	96	120	41	148	70
IN	53	18	25	42	68
IA	21	2	11	5	15
KS	2	24	49	4	46
KY	1	1	1	3	8
LA	44	155	67	17	17
ME	1	2	5	9	7
MD	31	85	74	38	84
MA	52	36	24	45	56
MI	14	30	42	36	22
MN	49	45	32	51	95
MS	10	6	12	12	9
MO	30	24	19	39	43
MT	0	0	0	0	0
NE	0	0	0	0	0

NV	0	0	0	0	0
NH	8	1	5	13	5
NJ	94	89	60	66	39
NM	0	0	0	0	0
NY	102	170	169	234	188
NC	95	59	55	128	56
ND	0	0	1	2	1
OH	83	32	55	57	117
OK	1	6	15	6	170
OR	38	24	70	13	4
PA	19	31	81	29	21
RI	0	0	0	0	0
SC	29	36	45	31	39
SD	0	0	0	0	0
TN	26	20	18	40	11
TX	169	152	70	126	64
UT	0	0	0	0	0
VT	0	0	0	0	0
VA	92	86	104	127	94
WA	33	12	3	38	17
WV	0	0	0	0	5
WI	48	37	38	56	130
WY	0	0	0	0	0
TOTAL	1827	1760	1633	1821	1894

Appendix - Direct US Manufacturing Jobs Generated by Exports to Lebanon (By Industry)

Jobs Generated	2001	2002	2003	2004	2005
311 Processed Foods	80	61	43	47	49
312 Beverage & Tobacco Products	43	22	21	28	30
313 Fabric Mill Products	37	19	22	16	13
314 Non-Apparel Textile Products	3	6	8	8	7
315 Apparel Manufactures	24	19	20	26	35
316 Leather & Related Products	9	7	10	10	5
321 Wood Products	25	37	17	22	18
322 Paper Products	31	25	25	35	30
323 Printing & Related Products	38	202	42	42	48
324 Petroleum & Coal Products	4	68	6	7	4
325 Chemical Manufactures	51	41	32	51	41
326 Plastic & Rubber Products	20	15	11	15	16
327 Non-Metallic Mineral Mfgs.	6	5	5	6	7
331 Primary Metal Manufactures	6	3	2	3	2
332 Fabricated Metal Products	50	30	22	32	45
333 Machinery Manufactures	102	72	78	93	100
334 Computers & Electronic Prod.	122	86	62	86	110
335 Elec. Eq., Appliances & Parts	102	85	81	176	159
336 Transportation Equipment	235	52	103	255	324
337 Furniture & Related Products	26	28	19	27	20
339 Misc. Manufactures	76	60	65	79	99
Total	1090	943	694	1063	1161

Appendix - Direct US Manufacturing Jobs Generated by Exports to Lebanon (By Origin of Movement)

	2001	2002	2003	2004	2005
AL	16	8	7	13	11
AK	0	0	0	0	0
AZ	2	2	2	2	2
AR	179	4	2	2	2
CA	115	80	83	146	140
CO	3	1	1	3	7
CT	6	5	4	8	9
DE	3	2	2	3	9
DC	0	0	0	0	0
FL	33	30	35	88	145
GA	21	29	25	34	30
HI	0	0	0	0	0
ID	0	0	0	0	0
IL	52	31	30	26	34
IN	14	15	12	25	17
IA	7	5	5	6	5
KS	3	3	3	5	5
KY	8	7	3	2	2
LA	21	16	6	12	12
ME	0	1	1	1	1
MD	32	16	15	13	18
MA	73	37	31	40	38
MI	38	19	30	50	50
MN	11	9	6	15	17
MS	5	6	5	5	7
MO	9	4	8	8	8
MT	0	0	0	0	0
NE	0	3	2	2	4
NV	9	6	0	0	0

NH	1	5	4	7	9
NJ	28	202	30	71	105
NM	0	0	0	0	0
NY	110	157	98	113	119
NC	43	39	22	46	45
ND	0	0	0	0	1
OH	35	48	34	108	69
OK	7	3	0	3	15
OR	3	3	3	4	5
PA	25	13	18	24	27
RI	2	1	1	1	1
SC	12	8	9	12	11
SD	1	1	0	1	0
TN	29	23	24	28	43
TX	49	42	51	72	68
UT	1	1	2	1	2
VT	0	0	0	0	0
VA	55	38	41	34	32
WA	8	7	8	5	8
WV	1	1	0	1	0
WI	18	14	32	24	28
WY	0	0	0	0	0
TOTAL	1090	943	694	1063	1161

Appendix - Direct and Indirect US Jobs Generated by Manufactures Exports to Lebanon (By Origin of Movement)

	2001	2002	2003	2004	2005
AL	49	23	20	38	32
AK	0	0	0	0	0
AZ	6	5	6	6	7
AR	538	13	5	6	7
CA	346	241	248	438	419
CO	8	3	4	8	20
CT	19	14	12	25	26
DE	9	6	7	9	26
DC	0	0	0	0	0
FL	98	89	105	264	436
GA	64	88	75	103	90
HI	0	0	0	0	0
ID	0	0	0	0	0
IL	155	93	91	79	101
IN	42	46	36	74	51
IA	22	16	14	17	14
KS	10	10	10	15	16
KY	24	22	8	5	5
LA	64	48	19	37	35
ME	1	3	3	2	2
MD	95	49	44	38	55
MA	219	111	93	119	113
MI	114	56	89	149	151
MN	33	26	17	45	52
MS	16	18	15	16	21
MO	27	13	24	23	24
MT	0	0	0	0	0
NE	0	8	5	6	11

NV	28	17	1	1	1
NH	2	14	12	22	26
NJ	83	607	91	213	316
NM	0	0	0	0	0
NY	331	470	294	338	358
NC	130	116	65	138	134
ND	0	0	1	0	4
OH	105	144	102	325	207
OK	20	8	1	10	45
OR	10	8	8	12	14
PA	74	39	54	71	80
RI	6	3	3	4	4
SC	35	24	27	35	33
SD	4	2	1	2	0
TN	86	70	71	85	128
TX	148	127	154	217	205
UT	2	2	5	4	7
VT	1	0	0	0	0
VA	164	113	122	103	97
WA	25	20	25	16	24
WV	2	2	0	2	1
WI	54	42	95	72	83
WY	0	0	0	0	0
TOTAL	3269	2829	2081	3190	3483

Appendix - Direct US Manufacturing Jobs Generated by Exports to Bahrain (By Industry)

Jobs Generated	2001	2002	2003	2004	2005
311 Processed Foods	62	50	34	35	32
312 Beverage & Tobacco Products	9	10	15	5	7
313 Fabric Mill Products	13	7	2	2	2
314 Non-Apparel Textile Products	10	4	4	6	4
315 Apparel Manufactures	10	8	5	6	5
316 Leather & Related Products	1	1	1	1	1
321 Wood Products	5	3	2	3	5
322 Paper Products	2	3	4	3	6
323 Printing & Related Products	13	21	18	20	23
324 Petroleum & Coal Products	6	2	0	1	0
325 Chemical Manufactures	18	17	16	13	16
326 Plastic & Rubber Products	10	11	12	9	12
327 Non-Metallic Mineral Mfgs.	9	3	7	5	9
331 Primary Metal Manufactures	26	8	10	10	5
332 Fabricated Metal Products	133	277	80	32	38
333 Machinery Manufactures	149	194	124	213	173
334 Computers & Electronic Prod.	110	75	105	96	85
335 Elec. Eq., Appliances & Parts	54	36	32	41	122
336 Transportation Equipment	402	283	220	224	253
337 Furniture & Related Products	46	37	28	20	23
339 Misc. Manufactures	34	30	24	36	34
Total	1120	1079	742	781	856

Appendix - Direct US Manufacturing Jobs Generated by Exports to Bahrain (By Origin of Movement)

	2001	2002	2003	2004	2005
AL	17	16	8	2	7
AK	0	0	0	0	0
AZ	87	131	3	43	4
AR	16	3	3	3	5
CA	87	108	101	41	68
CO	3	2	3	1	3
CT	4	4	8	5	4
DE	2	7	3	7	4
DC	0	0	0	0	0
FL	55	42	35	90	50
GA	40	41	20	11	15
HI	0	0	0	0	0
ID	0	1	0	0	0
IL	13	14	16	25	27
IN	9	5	10	6	6
IA	4	5	5	6	7
KS	4	11	2	4	4
KY	1	5	4	3	5
LA	3	11	6	3	6
ME	0	0	1	0	2
MD	130	184	73	42	25
MA	14	10	14	19	12
MI	57	46	43	28	39
MN	5	4	5	10	5
MS	16	10	7	7	21
MO	13	10	5	4	7
MT	0	0	0	0	0

NE	1	2	2	1	1
NV	1	0	1	1	2
NH	1	7	2	7	1
NJ	32	30	17	19	19
NM	0	0	0	0	0
NY	59	45	41	42	49
NC	34	39	53	29	56
ND	0	0	0	0	0
OH	29	47	39	49	67
OK	30	5	8	14	30
OR	1	6	3	2	14
PA	23	14	12	14	21
RI	1	0	0	1	1
SC	14	15	20	31	19
SD	0	1	0	0	0
TN	11	15	18	12	73
TX	155	57	81	74	78
UT	3	1	10	1	1
VT	0	0	0	0	0
VA	111	106	39	35	71
WA	22	9	10	67	15
WV	0	0	1	1	2
WI	9	9	13	17	8
WY	0	0	0	0	0
TOTAL	1120	1079	742	781	856

Appendix - Direct and Indirect US Jobs Generated by Manufactures Exports to Bahrain (By Origin of Movement)

	2001	2002	2003	2004	2005
AL	51	48	23	7	21
AK	0	0	0	0	0
AZ	262	393	8	129	12
AR	49	9	9	8	15
CA	261	324	303	122	205
CO	9	5	9	3	10
CT	11	13	25	16	12
DE	5	20	8	22	13
DC	0	0	0	0	0
FL	166	126	106	269	149
GA	120	123	60	34	46
HI	0	0	0	0	0
ID	0	4	0	0	1
IL	40	41	47	75	82
IN	26	14	30	19	19
IA	11	14	15	19	21
KS	12	34	5	12	13
KY	4	16	11	8	15
LA	9	33	18	10	17
ME	1	1	3	1	5
MD	391	553	218	125	74
MA	42	31	42	56	35
MI	172	137	128	83	117
MN	16	13	14	30	15
MS	49	31	22	22	64
MO	38	29	15	11	20
MT	0	0	0	0	0
NE	2	5	6	2	4

NV	3	1	3	4	5
NH	2	22	6	21	4
NJ	95	89	50	56	58
NM	1	1	0	0	0
NY	177	135	122	127	147
NC	103	117	159	88	169
ND	0	0	0	0	0
OH	87	141	117	148	201
OK	91	14	23	42	90
OR	4	19	10	5	41
PA	69	42	36	43	62
RI	2	1	1	2	4
SC	43	46	61	94	57
SD	0	3	0	0	0
TN	33	46	54	37	218
TX	465	172	242	223	233
UT	9	2	29	4	4
VT	1	0	0	0	0
VA	334	317	118	105	214
WA	65	26	31	202	45
WV	1	1	2	4	5
WI	27	26	40	51	25
WY	0	0	0	0	0
TOTAL	3361	3238	2226	2344	2567

Appendix - Direct US Manufacturing Jobs Generated by Exports to Tunisia (By Industry)

Jobs Generated	2001	2002	2003	2004	2005
311 Processed Foods	61	75	74	136	137
312 Beverage & Tobacco Products	4	1	0	0	0
313 Fabric Mill Products	8	4	3	4	10
314 Non-Apparel Textile Products	1	0	3	1	2
315 Apparel Manufactures	1	0	0	1	0
316 Leather & Related Products	1	1	8	1	0
321 Wood Products	1	2	1	2	3
322 Paper Products	6	11	21	22	22
323 Printing & Related Products	0	0	1	1	4
324 Petroleum & Coal Products	0	0	2	0	0
325 Chemical Manufactures	9	10	16	18	13
326 Plastic & Rubber Products	7	2	6	3	6
327 Non-Metallic Mineral Mfgs.	4	3	2	2	3
331 Primary Metal Manufactures	9	20	3	5	11
332 Fabricated Metal Products	21	22	6	10	38
333 Machinery Manufactures	159	174	91	117	174
334 Computers & Electronic Prod.	58	46	30	52	47
335 Elec. Eq., Appliances & Parts	61	25	15	8	10
336 Transportation Equipment	51	19	23	28	101
337 Furniture & Related Products	4	4	3	2	2
339 Misc. Manufactures	8	12	11	10	14
Total	476	431	319	423	598

Appendix - Direct US Jobs Generated by Manufactures Exports to Tunisia (By Origin of Movement)

	2001	2002	2003	2004	2005
AL	27	23	0	0	1
AK	0	0	0	0	0
AZ	2	2	0	3	2
AR	0	0	4	1	0
CA	48	19	33	33	102
CO	0	0	1	1	1
CT	2	2	5	6	4
DE	0	0	1	0	0
DC	0	0	0	0	0
FL	16	10	7	8	19
GA	11	12	12	16	19
HI	0	0	0	0	0
ID	0	0	0	0	0
IL	37	18	9	36	8
IN	2	1	1	4	5
IA	1	0	2	1	1
KS	1	1	1	1	8
KY	2	0	0	1	2
LA	49	82	72	126	200
ME	1	1	1	1	3
MD	17	3	8	5	3
MA	12	5	3	4	10
MI	1	2	1	2	4
MN	5	6	3	2	2
MS	1	0	0	1	0
MO	4	0	1	2	4
MT	0	0	0	0	0
NE	4	1	0	1	1
NV	0	0	0	0	0

NH	0	0	0	0	0
NJ	9	9	4	8	5
NM	0	0	0	0	0
NY	6	34	12	19	38
NC	5	6	5	6	4
ND	1	0	1	2	0
OH	7	5	6	10	16
OK	8	6	24	13	9
OR	1	0	0	1	1
PA	12	12	6	4	4
RI	0	2	0	0	0
SC	8	6	5	9	6
SD	0	0	0	0	0
TN	5	11	9	8	16
TX	137	113	50	58	74
UT	1	0	0	0	0
VT	0	0	0	0	0
VA	21	12	6	18	13
WA	2	3	2	2	0
WV	0	0	0	0	0
WI	8	20	26	10	12
WY	0	0	0	0	0
TOTAL	476	431	319	423	598

Appendix - Direct and Indirect US Jobs Generated by Manufactures Exports to Tunisia (By Origin of Movement)

	2001	2002	2003	2004	2005
AL	82	69	1	1	4
AK	0	0	0	0	0
AZ	7	5	1	10	6
AR	1	1	11	2	0
CA	144	58	100	99	305
CO	0	1	2	3	2
CT	7	6	16	17	11
DE	0	0	2	0	0
DC	0	0	0	0	0
FL	49	29	21	24	56
GA	32	36	35	49	57
HI	0	0	0	0	0
ID	0	0	0	0	0
IL	111	53	26	108	25
IN	7	3	2	12	15
IA	3	0	5	3	2
KS	3	4	2	4	23
KY	5	1	0	3	6
LA	147	246	216	377	600
ME	3	2	3	4	8
MD	52	10	23	15	8
MA	37	16	10	12	31
MI	3	7	4	7	13
MN	14	18	8	7	7
MS	3	1	1	3	1
MO	11	1	2	6	12
MT	0	0	0	0	0
NE	13	2	1	4	2
NV	0	1	0	0	1

NH	1	0	0	0	0
NJ	28	28	12	23	15
NM	0	0	0	0	0
NY	19	102	35	56	115
NC	16	18	15	17	11
ND	3	1	3	6	0
OH	20	15	18	29	47
OK	23	19	73	38	27
OR	2	1	1	2	2
PA	35	36	17	12	11
RI	0	5	1	1	0
SC	23	19	16	26	19
SD	0	1	0	0	0
TN	16	32	27	25	48
TX	410	339	149	173	222
UT	2	1	0	1	1
VT	0	0	0	0	0
VA	64	36	17	53	40
WA	7	9	5	7	1
WV	0	1	1	0	0
WI	24	59	78	30	36
WY	0	0	0	0	0
TOTAL	1427	1294	957	1268	1793

Appendix - Direct US Manufacturing Jobs Generated by Exports to Yemen (By Industry)

Jobs Generated	2001	2002	2003	2004	2005
311 Processed Foods	59	82	51	89	29
312 Beverage & Tobacco Products	0	0	0	0	0
313 Fabric Mill Products	0	0	0	0	0
314 Non-Apparel Textile Products	2	1	0	0	0
315 Apparel Manufactures	0	0	0	0	0
316 Leather & Related Products	0	0	0	1	0
321 Wood Products	0	0	0	0	0
322 Paper Products	5	7	10	12	21
323 Printing & Related Products	0	0	0	0	1
324 Petroleum & Coal Products	0	0	0	0	0
325 Chemical Manufactures	8	9	8	8	8
326 Plastic & Rubber Products	4	5	6	4	5
327 Non-Metallic Mineral Mfgs.	6	3	6	2	7
331 Primary Metal Manufactures	3	4	5	8	7
332 Fabricated Metal Products	10	15	47	49	46
333 Machinery Manufactures	222	223	196	137	244
334 Computers & Electronic Prod.	34	29	29	50	36
335 Elec. Eq., Appliances & Parts	38	103	113	74	72
336 Transportation Equipment	40	13	24	11	28
337 Furniture & Related Products	5	2	3	1	0
339 Misc. Manufactures	6	5	5	15	7
Total	441	503	506	463	511

Appendix - Direct US Manufacturing Jobs Generated by Exports to Yemen (By Origin of Movement)

	2001	2002	2003	2004	2005
AL	1	3	1	0	2
AK	0	0	0	0	0
AZ	31	0	2	4	3
AR	4	2	5	13	7
CA	27	49	30	48	32
CO	0	3	1	4	1
CT	1	1	2	1	3
DE	0	1	0	0	0
DC	0	0	0	0	0
FL	2	3	6	3	3
GA	13	8	12	22	5
HI	0	0	0	0	0
ID	0	0	0	0	0
IL	7	29	29	30	39
IN	7	27	27	29	35
IA	3	5	2	1	1
KS	9	18	8	8	7
KY	0	0	1	1	1
LA	5	6	7	6	6
ME	0	1	0	0	0
MD	5	1	2	3	3
MA	13	11	8	14	10
MI	2	1	3	4	6
MN	1	5	4	1	5
MS	6	0	1	1	3
MO	0	1	4	16	1
MT	0	0	0	0	0
NE	5	0	0	0	17
NV	0	0	0	0	0

NH	2	6	0	0	3
NJ	8	4	2	2	4
NM	0	0	0	0	0
NY	6	5	7	2	11
NC	1	7	8	2	1
ND	0	0	0	0	0
OH	4	5	7	10	7
OK	12	53	30	19	13
OR	0	1	1	0	0
PA	10	11	11	8	4
RI	0	0	0	0	0
SC	1	1	5	4	8
SD	0	0	0	0	0
TN	1	2	1	4	2
TX	232	224	270	188	251
UT	0	2	1	0	0
VT	0	0	0	0	0
VA	2	2	4	3	8
WA	1	2	1	6	1
WV	0	0	0	0	0
WI	19	3	3	3	7
WY	0	0	0	0	0
TOTAL	441	503	506	463	511

Appendix - Direct and Indirect US Jobs Generated by Manufactures Exports to Yemen (By Origin of Movement)

	2001	2002	2003	2004	2005
AL	2	10	4	1	6
AK	0	0	0	0	0
AZ	92	1	6	12	10
AR	13	7	14	39	22
CA	81	146	89	143	95
CO	0	8	4	11	3
CT	4	3	5	2	9
DE	1	2	0	1	1
DC	0	0	0	0	0
FL	6	8	17	9	8
GA	39	25	36	66	14
HI	0	0	0	0	0
ID	0	0	0	0	0
IL	21	87	86	90	117
IN	21	82	81	87	106
IA	8	14	6	3	3
KS	28	53	24	25	20
KY	1	1	4	3	4
LA	14	19	21	19	19
ME	0	2	0	0	0
MD	15	4	5	10	8
MA	39	34	25	41	29
MI	6	2	10	13	17
MN	2	14	11	3	14
MS	18	1	2	2	8
MO	1	3	13	49	3
MT	0	0	0	0	0
NE	16	0	1	1	52
NV	0	0	0	0	0

NH	5	17	1	1	9
NJ	23	11	6	7	11
NM	0	0	0	0	0
NY	17	15	20	7	32
NC	4	22	23	6	2
ND	0	1	0	0	1
OH	11	15	22	30	22
OK	36	158	91	56	39
OR	0	2	4	1	1
PA	31	33	32	23	11
RI	0	1	0	0	1
SC	3	2	15	13	24
SD	0	0	0	0	0
TN	2	5	4	12	5
TX	696	672	810	563	753
UT	0	7	2	0	1
VT	0	0	0	0	1
VA	7	6	12	9	25
WA	2	6	3	19	4
WV	0	0	0	0	0
WI	56	9	8	10	22
WY	0	0	0	0	0
TOTAL	1323	1510	1518	1389	1533

Appendix - Direct US Manufacturing Jobs Generated by Exports to Syria (By Industry)

Jobs Generated	2001	2002	2003	2004	2005
311 Processed Foods	42	32	10	13	20
312 Beverage & Tobacco Products	21	10	5	2	0
313 Fabric Mill Products	69	33	10	2	0
314 Non-Apparel Textile Products	1	2	3	1	0
315 Apparel Manufactures	0	0	0	0	0
316 Leather & Related Products	0	1	2	0	0
321 Wood Products	12	17	16	8	0
322 Paper Products	20	12	20	18	0
323 Printing & Related Products	1	1	4	1	1
324 Petroleum & Coal Products	0	0	0	0	0
325 Chemical Manufactures	44	37	34	20	6
326 Plastic & Rubber Products	9	14	7	5	12
327 Non-Metallic Mineral Mfgs.	4	6	3	1	0
331 Primary Metal Manufactures	9	3	2	0	0
332 Fabricated Metal Products	11	9	11	4	0
333 Machinery Manufactures	223	321	193	62	1
334 Computers & Electronic Prod.	29	38	37	20	9
335 Elec. Eq., Appliances & Parts	21	31	19	6	0
336 Transportation Equipment	25	28	29	58	0
337 Furniture & Related Products	1	2	3	3	0
339 Misc. Manufactures	11	16	22	14	6
Total	551	613	429	238	57

Appendix - Direct US Manufacturing Jobs Generated by Exports to Syria (By Origin of Movement)

	2001	2002	2003	2004	2005
AL	4	17	24	1	0
AK	0	0	0	0	0
AZ	1	0	0	1	0
AR	0	1	1	0	0
CA	41	27	27	17	15
CO	0	1	0	1	1
CT	3	5	1	0	0
DE	8	7	2	0	0
DC	0	0	0	0	0
FL	5	5	19	10	1
GA	24	22	17	7	3
HI	0	0	0	0	0
ID	0	0	0	0	0
IL	15	7	5	6	2
IN	4	10	3	3	2
IA	3	1	1	1	0
KS	5	3	2	0	0
KY	3	2	0	1	0
LA	7	10	1	13	6
ME	0	1	2	0	0
MD	6	3	2	1	0
MA	5	6	9	5	1
MI	12	7	19	6	0
MN	2	2	2	5	13
MS	0	1	1	0	0
MO	5	2	2	0	0
MT	0	0	0	0	0
NE	0	5	1	1	0
NV	0	0	0	0	0

NH	14	4	3	0	0
NJ	22	14	10	9	2
NM	0	0	0	0	0
NY	25	20	27	13	1
NC	68	39	21	12	0
ND	1	2	0	0	0
OH	16	9	21	3	0
OK	12	21	22	7	0
OR	0	1	4	0	0
PA	52	62	12	3	1
RI	1	1	0	1	0
SC	20	15	7	3	2
SD	0	0	0	0	0
TN	3	2	3	1	1
TX	136	246	139	52	1
UT	1	0	1	0	0
VT	2	2	2	0	0
VA	14	12	7	11	0
WA	3	5	2	1	0
WV	0	0	0	0	0
WI	7	11	7	42	3
WY	0	0	0	0	0
TOTAL	551	613	429	238	57

Appendix - Direct and Indirect US Jobs Generated by Manufactures Exports to Syria (By Origin of Movement)

	2001	2002	2003	2004	2005
AL	11	51	72	4	0
AK	0	0	0	0	0
AZ	3	0	1	2	0
AR	1	2	3	0	0
CA	122	80	80	51	46
CO	1	4	0	3	2
CT	10	16	3	0	0
DE	25	20	6	0	0
DC	0	0	0	0	0
FL	14	16	58	29	4
GA	73	65	50	20	10
HI	0	0	0	0	0
ID	0	0	0	0	0
IL	44	22	16	19	5
IN	13	31	10	9	7
IA	9	2	2	4	0
KS	16	9	7	0	0
KY	9	6	1	2	0
LA	21	30	3	40	18
ME	1	3	5	0	0
MD	19	8	7	2	1
MA	16	17	28	14	3
MI	37	20	56	17	0
MN	5	6	5	16	38
MS	1	2	3	1	1
MO	15	7	5	1	0
MT	0	0	0	0	0
NE	0	14	2	4	0
NV	0	1	0	0	0

NH	42	13	9	1	0
NJ	65	42	30	27	7
NM	0	0	1	0	0
NY	74	61	80	39	3
NC	204	118	64	35	1
ND	3	5	0	0	0
OH	48	28	62	9	1
OK	35	64	66	22	0
OR	1	4	11	0	0
PA	155	185	35	10	4
RI	2	2	1	2	0
SC	60	46	21	10	5
SD	0	0	0	0	0
TN	8	6	9	3	3
TX	407	739	418	157	2
UT	2	1	2	0	0
VT	7	5	5	1	0
VA	43	36	22	32	0
WA	8	16	5	3	0
WV	0	0	0	1	0
WI	20	34	22	125	9
WY	0	1	0	0	0
TOTAL	1653	1839	1288	714	171

Appendix - Direct US Manufacturing Jobs Generated by Exports to Sudan (By Industry)

Jobs Generated	2001	2002	2003	2004	2005
311 Processed Foods	14	10	31	67	60
312 Beverage & Tobacco Products	0	0	0	0	0
313 Fabric Mill Products	0	0	0	0	0
314 Non-Apparel Textile Products	0	0	0	2	13
315 Apparel Manufactures	0	0	0	0	0
316 Leather & Related Products	0	0	0	0	0
321 Wood Products	0	0	0	0	0
322 Paper Products	0	0	0	0	1
323 Printing & Related Products	0	1	0	0	0
324 Petroleum & Coal Products	0	0	0	0	0
325 Chemical Manufactures	0	1	1	8	2
326 Plastic & Rubber Products	0	0	0	0	0
327 Non-Metallic Mineral Mfgs.	0	0	0	0	0
331 Primary Metal Manufactures	0	0	0	0	0
332 Fabricated Metal Products	0	0	0	0	0
333 Machinery Manufactures	1	0	0	0	0
334 Computers & Electronic Prod.	0	0	0	1	8
335 Elec. Eq., Appliances & Parts	0	0	0	0	0
336 Transportation Equipment	0	0	0	4	0
337 Furniture & Related Products	0	0	0	0	0
339 Misc. Manufactures	0	0	0	0	1
Total	15	12	34	83	87

Appendix - Direct US Manufacturing Jobs Generated by Exports to Sudan (By Origin of Movement)

	2001	2002	2003	2004	2005
AL	0	0	0	0	0
AK	0	0	0	0	0
AZ	0	0	0	0	0
AR	0	0	0	0	0
CA	0	0	0	0	1
CO	0	0	0	0	0
CT	0	0	0	0	0
DE	0	0	0	0	0
DC	0	0	0	0	0
FL	0	0	5	0	0
GA	0	0	0	0	0
HI	0	0	0	0	0
ID	0	0	0	0	0
IL	0	0	0	0	1
IN	0	0	0	0	0
IA	0	0	0	0	0
KS	2	0	0	0	1
KY	0	0	0	0	0
LA	5	2	5	13	2
ME	0	0	0	0	0
MD	0	0	0	0	0
MA	0	0	0	1	0
MI	0	0	1	0	1
MN	0	0	0	0	0
MS	1	0	0	0	0
MO	0	2	1	1	0
MT	0	0	0	0	0
NE	0	1	1	0	0
NV	0	0	0	0	0

NH	0	0	0	0	0
NJ	0	0	0	7	31
NM	0	0	0	0	0
NY	0	4	1	8	6
NC	0	0	0	0	2
ND	0	0	0	0	0
OH	0	0	0	0	2
OK	0	0	0	0	0
OR	0	0	0	0	1
PA	0	0	0	0	0
RI	0	0	0	0	0
SC	0	1	0	8	8
SD	0	0	0	0	0
TN	1	0	9	0	3
TX	3	2	3	15	14
UT	0	0	0	0	0
VT	0	0	0	0	0
VA	0	0	1	28	3
WA	2	0	1	0	3
WV	0	0	0	0	0
WI	1	0	5	0	8
WY	0	0	0	0	0
TOTAL	15	12	34	83	87

Appendix - Direct and Indirect US Jobs Generated by Manufactures Exports to Sudan (By Origin of Movement)

	2001	2002	2003	2004	2005
AL	0	0	0	0	0
AK	0	0	0	0	0
AZ	0	0	0	0	0
AR	0	0	0	0	0
CA	0	0	1	0	4
CO	0	0	0	0	0
CT	0	0	0	0	0
DE	0	0	0	0	0
DC	0	0	0	0	0
FL	1	0	14	1	1
GA	0	1	1	0	1
HI	0	0	0	0	0
ID	0	0	0	0	0
IL	0	0	0	0	2
IN	0	0	0	0	0
IA	0	0	0	0	0
KS	5	0	0	0	2
KY	0	0	0	0	0
LA	16	6	16	38	5
ME	0	0	0	0	0
MD	0	0	1	0	0
MA	0	0	0	3	0
MI	0	0	2	0	2
MN	0	0	0	1	0
MS	2	0	0	0	0
MO	0	7	4	2	0
MT	0	0	0	0	0
NE	0	4	4	0	1
NV	0	0	0	0	0

NH	0	0	0	0	0
NJ	0	0	1	22	93
NM	0	0	0	0	0
NY	1	11	4	25	18
NC	0	0	0	1	6
ND	0	0	0	0	0
OH	0	0	0	0	5
OK	0	0	0	0	0
OR	0	0	0	0	2
PA	0	0	0	0	0
RI	0	0	0	0	0
SC	0	2	0	24	24
SD	0	0	0	0	0
TN	3	0	26	1	10
TX	8	6	8	46	41
UT	0	0	0	0	0
VT	0	0	0	0	0
VA	1	0	2	84	10
WA	5	0	3	0	8
WV	0	0	0	0	0
WI	2	0	15	0	24
WY	0	0	0	0	0
TOTAL	45	37	103	249	261

Appendix - Direct US Manufacturing Jobs Generated by Exports to Mauritania (By Industry)

Jobs Generated	2001	2002	2003	2004	2005
311 Processed Foods	6	3	13	10	9
312 Beverage & Tobacco Products	0	0	1	1	1
313 Fabric Mill Products	1	2	3	5	4
314 Non-Apparel Textile Products	0	0	3	3	4
315 Apparel Manufactures	0	0	2	2	2
316 Leather & Related Products	0	0	3	3	3
321 Wood Products	0	0	2	2	2
322 Paper Products	0	0	2	2	2
323 Printing & Related Products	0	0	2	2	2
324 Petroleum & Coal Products	0	0	1	1	5
325 Chemical Manufactures	0	1	2	10	8
326 Plastic & Rubber Products	0	1	2	2	7
327 Non-Metallic Mineral Mfgs.	1	0	2	2	2
331 Primary Metal Manufactures	8	1	3	2	2
332 Fabricated Metal Products	3	1	3	6	6
333 Machinery Manufactures	70	70	68	74	131
334 Computers & Electronic Prod.	10	4	15	8	9
335 Elec. Eq., Appliances & Parts	0	0	3	2	19
336 Transportation Equipment	1	0	2	154	26
337 Furniture & Related Products	0	0	2	2	2
339 Misc. Manufactures	0	0	2	2	2
Total	100	83	136	293	247

Appendix - Direct US Manufacturing Jobs Generated by Exports to Mauritania (By Origin of Movement)

	2001	2002	2003	2004	2005
AL	0	0	0	0	0
AK	0	0	0	0	0
AZ	3	1	2	3	20
AR	0	0	1	2	2
CA	6	1	11	154	3
CO	0	0	0	0	0
CT	0	0	0	0	0
DE	0	0	0	0	0
DC	0	0	0	0	0
FL	2	0	1	1	3
GA	2	0	2	0	0
HI	0	0	0	0	0
ID	0	0	0	0	0
IL	0	0	20	19	19
IN	0	0	17	16	16
IA	1	0	0	0	0
KS	0	0	2	0	4
KY	0	1	1	2	1
LA	0	2	0	0	3
ME	0	0	0	0	0
MD	0	0	0	2	0
MA	0	1	0	0	0
MI	1	0	0	0	1
MN	5	1	2	0	11
MS	0	0	0	0	0
MO	4	0	0	0	1
MT	0	0	0	0	0
NE	0	0	0	0	0
NV	0	0	0	0	0

NH	0	0	0	0	0
NJ	2	2	4	9	13
NM	0	0	0	0	0
NY	5	3	4	12	17
NC	1	0	1	1	1
ND	0	0	0	0	0
OH	0	2	8	4	4
OK	2	3	3	8	8
OR	0	0	0	0	0
PA	1	1	1	1	4
RI	0	0	0	0	0
SC	1	1	2	2	3
SD	0	0	0	0	0
TN	2	0	0	0	0
TX	15	12	19	39	80
UT	0	0	0	0	0
VT	0	0	0	0	0
VA	0	0	2	1	0
WA	0	0	0	0	0
WV	0	0	0	0	0
WI	47	51	32	17	33
WY	0	0	0	0	0
TOTAL	100	83	136	293	247

Appendix - Direct and Indirect US Jobs Generated by Manufactures Exports to Mauritania (By Origin of Movement)

	2001	2002	2003	2004	2005
AL	0	0	0	0	0
AK	0	0	0	0	0
AZ	10	4	5	9	60
AR	0	0	2	5	6
CA	19	4	33	462	9
CO	0	0	0	0	0
CT	0	0	0	0	0
DE	0	0	0	0	0
DC	0	0	0	0	0
FL	5	1	3	2	8
GA	5	0	5	1	0
HI	0	0	0	0	0
ID	0	0	0	0	0
IL	0	0	60	57	57
IN	0	0	51	48	48
IA	2	0	0	0	0
KS	0	0	6	0	12
KY	1	2	2	6	2
LA	1	5	0	1	9
ME	0	1	0	0	1
MD	0	0	0	7	0
MA	1	4	1	1	1
MI	2	0	1	1	2
MN	16	4	5	0	32
MS	0	0	0	0	0
MO	11	0	0	1	2
MT	0	0	0	0	0
NE	0	0	0	0	0
NV	0	0	0	0	0

NH	0	0	0	0	0
NJ	5	7	13	26	39
NM	0	0	0	0	0
NY	15	10	13	37	51
NC	2	0	2	2	2
ND	0	0	0	0	0
OH	1	5	24	11	13
OK	6	8	10	25	24
OR	0	0	0	0	0
PA	3	2	4	4	13
RI	0	0	0	0	0
SC	2	3	5	5	8
SD	0	0	0	0	0
TN	7	0	1	0	1
TX	44	36	57	117	239
UT	0	0	0	0	0
VT	0	0	0	0	0
VA	0	1	5	3	1
WA	0	0	0	0	0
WV	0	0	0	0	0
WI	141	154	97	50	98
WY	0	0	0	0	0
TOTAL	299	250	407	880	740

Appendix - Direct US Manufacturing Jobs Generated by Exports to Libya (By Industry)

Jobs Generated	2001	2002	2003	2004	2005
311 Processed Foods	0	0	1	3	2
312 Beverage & Tobacco Products	0	0	0	0	0
313 Fabric Mill Products	0	0	0	0	0
314 Non-Apparel Textile Products	0	0	0	0	0
315 Apparel Manufactures	0	0	0	0	0
316 Leather & Related Products	0	0	0	0	0
321 Wood Products	0	0	0	0	0
322 Paper Products	0	0	0	0	0
323 Printing & Related Products	0	0	0	0	0
324 Petroleum & Coal Products	0	0	0	0	0
325 Chemical Manufactures	0	0	0	5	7
326 Plastic & Rubber Products	0	0	0	0	6
327 Non-Metallic Mineral Mfgs.	0	0	0	0	0
331 Primary Metal Manufactures	0	0	0	0	3
332 Fabricated Metal Products	0	0	0	2	8
333 Machinery Manufactures	0	0	0	76	158
334 Computers & Electronic Prod.	0	0	0	12	39
335 Elec. Eq., Appliances & Parts	0	0	0	2	8
336 Transportation Equipment	0	0	0	1	45
337 Furniture & Related Products	0	0	0	0	0
339 Misc. Manufactures	0	0	0	5	2
Total	0	0	1	108	278

Appendix - Direct US Manufacturing Jobs Generated by Exports to Libya (By Origin of Movement)

	2001	2002	2003	2004	2005
AL	0	0	0	0	0
AK	0	0	0	0	0
AZ	0	0	0	0	0
AR	0	0	0	0	0
CA	0	0	0	6	9
CO	0	0	0	0	2
CT	0	0	0	0	0
DE	0	0	0	0	0
DC	0	0	0	0	0
FL	0	0	0	0	13
GA	0	0	0	0	3
HI	0	0	0	0	0
ID	0	0	0	0	0
IL	0	0	0	1	5
IN	0	0	0	0	0
IA	0	0	0	1	0
KS	0	0	0	0	1
KY	0	0	0	0	0
LA	0	0	0	0	5
ME	0	0	0	0	1
MD	0	0	0	0	0
MA	0	0	0	1	10
MI	0	0	0	0	0
MN	0	0	0	0	2
MS	0	0	1	1	0
MO	0	0	0	0	4
MT	0	0	0	0	0
NE	0	0	0	1	7
NV	0	0	0	0	0

NH	0	0	0	0	1
NJ	0	0	0	0	3
NM	0	0	0	0	1
NY	0	0	0	0	3
NC	0	0	0	5	11
ND	0	0	0	0	1
OH	0	0	0	7	6
OK	0	0	0	3	10
OR	0	0	0	0	0
PA	0	0	0	0	6
RI	0	0	0	0	0
SC	0	0	0	0	0
SD	0	0	0	0	0
TN	0	0	0	0	0
TX	0	0	0	79	169
UT	0	0	0	0	0
VT	0	0	0	0	0
VA	0	0	0	0	1
WA	0	0	0	0	0
WV	0	0	0	0	0
WI	0	0	0	0	1
WY	0	0	0	0	0
TOTAL	0	0	1	108	278

Appendix - Direct and Indirect US Jobs Generated by Manufactures Exports to Libya (By Origin of Movement)

	2001	2002	2003	2004	2005
AL	0	0	0	0	0
AK	0	0	0	0	0
AZ	0	0	0	0	0
AR	0	0	0	1	0
CA	0	0	0	19	26
CO	0	0	0	0	7
CT	0	0	0	0	1
DE	0	0	0	0	0
DC	0	0	0	0	0
FL	0	0	0	1	38
GA	0	0	0	0	9
HI	0	0	0	0	0
ID	0	0	0	0	0
IL	0	0	0	2	16
IN	0	0	0	0	1
IA	0	0	0	2	1
KS	0	0	0	0	3
KY	0	0	0	0	1
LA	0	0	0	1	16
ME	0	0	0	0	3
MD	0	0	0	1	1
MA	0	0	0	4	30
MI	0	0	0	0	1
MN	0	0	0	0	6
MS	0	0	3	2	0
MO	0	0	0	0	11
MT	0	0	0	0	0
NE	0	0	0	4	20
NV	0	0	0	0	0

NH	0	0	0	0	2
NJ	0	0	0	1	10
NM	0	0	0	0	3
NY	0	0	0	1	9
NC	0	0	0	14	32
ND	0	0	0	0	3
OH	0	0	0	22	19
OK	0	0	0	10	30
OR	0	0	0	0	0
PA	0	0	0	0	18
RI	0	0	0	0	0
SC	0	0	0	0	0
SD	0	0	0	0	1
TN	0	0	0	0	1
TX	0	0	0	238	508
UT	0	0	0	0	1
VT	0	0	0	0	0
VA	0	0	0	1	4
WA	0	0	0	0	0
WV	0	0	0	0	0
WI	0	0	0	0	2
WY	0	0	0	0	0
TOTAL	0	0	3	323	833

Appendix - Direct US Manufacturing Jobs Generated by Exports to Djibouti (By Industry)

Jobs Generated	2001	2002	2003	2004	2005
311 Processed Foods	3	16	7	19	13
312 Beverage & Tobacco Products	0	0	0	0	0
313 Fabric Mill Products	0	0	0	0	0
314 Non-Apparel Textile Products	0	0	0	0	2
315 Apparel Manufactures	0	0	0	0	1
316 Leather & Related Products	0	0	0	0	0
321 Wood Products	0	0	0	0	3
322 Paper Products	0	0	1	0	0
323 Printing & Related Products	0	26	34	0	1
324 Petroleum & Coal Products	0	0	0	0	0
325 Chemical Manufactures	1	0	3	1	3
326 Plastic & Rubber Products	1	0	2	0	0
327 Non-Metallic Mineral Mfgs.	0	0	0	0	0
331 Primary Metal Manufactures	0	0	0	1	0
332 Fabricated Metal Products	3	1	0	1	1
333 Machinery Manufactures	2	2	4	14	17
334 Computers & Electronic Prod.	0	6	10	4	12
335 Elec. Eq., Appliances & Parts	1	1	0	1	2
336 Transportation Equipment	1	12	1	1	4
337 Furniture & Related Products	0	0	0	0	0
339 Misc. Manufactures	0	0	1	0	0
Total	13	66	64	41	58

Appendix - Direct US Manufacturing Jobs Generated by Exports to Djibouti (By Origin of Movement)

	2001	2002	2003	2004	2005
AL	0	0	0	0	0
AK	0	0	0	0	0
AZ	0	0	0	0	3
AR	0	1	4	1	1
CA	0	11	1	2	1
CO	0	0	0	0	0
CT	0	0	1	0	0
DE	0	0	0	0	0
DC	0	0	0	0	0
FL	1	1	2	4	1
GA	0	2	35	2	1
HI	0	0	0	0	0
ID	0	0	0	0	0
IL	1	0	0	1	1
IN	0	0	0	1	0
IA	0	0	0	1	0
KS	0	1	0	0	0
KY	0	0	0	0	0
LA	4	2	0	8	2
ME	0	0	0	0	0
MD	0	2	6	0	8
MA	2	2	2	3	2
MI	0	0	0	0	0
MN	1	0	0	0	0
MS	0	1	0	0	0
MO	0	0	0	0	0
MT	0	0	0	0	0
NE	0	0	0	1	0
NV	0	0	0	0	0

NH	0	0	0	0	0
NJ	0	6	0	8	16
NM	0	0	0	0	0
NY	2	11	3	0	2
NC	0	0	5	0	1
ND	0	0	0	0	0
OH	0	0	0	0	0
OK	0	0	0	0	12
OR	0	0	1	0	0
PA	0	0	1	1	1
RI	0	0	0	0	0
SC	0	0	2	0	0
SD	0	0	0	0	0
TN	0	0	0	0	1
TX	0	0	0	0	0
UT	0	0	0	0	0
VT	0	0	0	0	0
VA	1	26	1	7	3
WA	0	0	1	0	1
WV	0	0	0	0	0
WI	0	0	0	0	0
WY	0	0	0	0	0
TOTAL	13	66	64	41	58

Appendix - Direct and Indirect US Jobs Generated by Manufactures Exports to Djibouti (By Origin of Movement)

	2001	2002	2003	2004	2005
AL	0	0	0	0	0
AK	0	0	0	0	0
AZ	0	0	0	0	8
AR	1	2	11	2	2
CA	0	33	3	6	4
CO	0	0	0	0	0
CT	0	1	2	0	1
DE	0	0	0	0	0
DC	0	0	0	0	0
FL	2	3	5	11	4
GA	1	6	104	7	3
HI	0	0	0	0	0
ID	0	0	0	0	0
IL	3	1	0	3	2
IN	0	0	0	3	0
IA	0	0	0	4	0
KS	0	2	0	0	1
KY	0	0	0	0	0
LA	11	5	0	23	6
ME	0	0	0	0	0
MD	1	6	17	1	25
MA	5	6	7	9	6
MI	0	0	1	0	1
MN	2	0	0	0	1
MS	0	2	0	1	0
MO	0	0	0	0	0
MT	0	0	0	0	0
NE	0	0	0	2	1
NV	0	0	0	0	0

NH	0	0	0	0	0
NJ	1	19	1	25	49
NM	0	0	0	0	0
NY	5	34	9	1	5
NC	1	1	14	1	3
ND	0	0	0	0	0
OH	1	0	1	1	0
OK	0	0	0	1	36
OR	0	0	2	0	0
PA	1	0	2	2	3
RI	0	0	0	0	0
SC	0	0	7	1	1
SD	0	0	0	0	0
TN	1	0	0	1	2
TX	0	0	0	0	0
UT	0	0	0	0	0
VT	0	0	0	0	0
VA	4	77	3	20	8
WA	0	0	2	0	3
WV	0	0	0	0	0
WI	0	0	1	0	1
WY	0	0	0	0	0
TOTAL	40	197	192	124	175

Appendix - Direct US Manufacturing Jobs Generated by Exports to Somalia (By Industry)

Jobs Generated	2001	2002	2003	2004	2005
311 Processed Foods	5	2	7	9	4
312 Beverage & Tobacco Products	0	0	0	0	0
313 Fabric Mill Products	1	0	2	2	2
314 Non-Apparel Textile Products	0	0	2	3	2
315 Apparel Manufactures	1	0	1	1	1
316 Leather & Related Products	0	0	1	1	1
321 Wood Products	0	0	4	3	3
322 Paper Products	0	0	2	2	2
323 Printing & Related Products	0	0	2	2	2
324 Petroleum & Coal Products	0	0	2	2	2
325 Chemical Manufactures	0	0	3	5	3
326 Plastic & Rubber Products	0	0	2	2	2
327 Non-Metallic Mineral Mfgs.	0	0	2	2	2
331 Primary Metal Manufactures	0	0	3	3	3
332 Fabricated Metal Products	0	0	2	2	2
333 Machinery Manufactures	0	0	3	5	2
334 Computers & Electronic Prod.	3	11	5	3	11
335 Elec. Eq., Appliances & Parts	0	0	2	2	2
336 Transportation Equipment	2	0	2	2	2
337 Furniture & Related Products	0	1	3	3	3
339 Misc. Manufactures	0	0	3	3	3
Total	12	14	54	56	54

Appendix - Direct US Manufacturing Jobs Generated by Exports to Somalia (By Origin of Movement)

	2001	2002	2003	2004	2005
AL	0	0	0	0	0
AK	0	0	0	0	0
AZ	0	0	0	0	0
AR	0	0	0	0	0
CA	2	2	0	1	0
CO	0	0	0	0	0
CT	0	0	0	0	0
DE	0	0	0	0	0
DC	0	0	0	0	0
FL	2	9	2	1	7
GA	0	0	0	0	0
HI	0	0	0	0	0
ID	0	0	0	0	0
IL	1	0	0	0	0
IN	0	0	0	0	0
IA	0	0	0	0	0
KS	0	0	0	2	0
KY	0	0	0	0	0
LA	2	0	0	2	1
ME	0	0	0	0	0
MD	0	1	1	0	1
MA	0	0	0	0	0
MI	0	0	0	0	0
MN	0	0	1	5	0
MS	1	0	0	0	0
MO	1	1	4	0	0
MT	0	0	0	0	0
NE	0	0	0	0	0
NV	0	0	0	0	0

NH	0	0	0	0	0
NJ	0	0	0	0	0
NM	0	0	0	0	0
NY	0	0	15	14	14
NC	0	0	6	6	6
ND	0	0	0	0	0
OH	0	0	22	21	21
OK	0	0	0	0	0
OR	0	0	0	0	0
PA	0	0	0	0	0
RI	0	0	0	0	0
SC	0	0	0	0	0
SD	0	0	0	0	0
TN	0	0	1	0	1
TX	2	1	1	5	2
UT	0	0	0	0	0
VT	0	0	0	0	0
VA	0	0	0	0	0
WA	0	0	0	0	0
WV	0	0	0	0	0
WI	0	0	0	0	0
WY	0	0	0	0	0
TOTAL	12	14	54	56	54

Appendix - Direct and Indirect US Jobs Generated by Manufactures Exports to Somalia (By Origin of Movement)

	2001	2002	2003	2004	2005
AL	0	0	0	0	0
AK	0	0	0	0	0
AZ	0	0	0	0	1
AR	0	0	0	0	0
CA	5	7	1	2	0
CO	0	0	0	0	0
CT	0	0	0	0	0
DE	0	0	0	0	0
DC	0	0	0	0	0
FL	5	26	7	2	21
GA	1	0	0	0	0
HI	0	0	0	0	0
ID	0	0	0	0	0
IL	3	0	0	0	1
IN	0	0	0	0	0
IA	0	0	0	0	0
KS	0	0	0	5	0
KY	0	0	0	0	0
LA	7	0	0	5	2
ME	0	0	0	0	0
MD	1	2	2	0	3
MA	0	0	0	0	0
MI	0	0	0	0	0
MN	0	0	2	14	0
MS	2	0	0	0	0
MO	4	4	13	1	1
MT	0	0	0	0	0
NE	0	0	0	0	1
NV	0	0	0	0	0

NH	0	0	0	0	0
NJ	0	0	0	0	1
NM	0	0	0	0	0
NY	0	0	45	43	43
NC	0	0	19	18	19
ND	0	0	0	0	0
OH	1	0	65	62	62
OK	0	0	0	0	0
OR	0	0	0	0	0
PA	0	0	0	0	0
RI	0	0	0	0	0
SC	0	0	1	0	0
SD	0	0	0	0	0
TN	0	0	2	0	2
TX	5	3	3	16	5
UT	0	0	0	0	0
VT	0	0	0	0	0
VA	0	0	1	0	0
WA	0	0	0	0	0
WV	0	0	0	0	0
WI	0	0	0	0	0
WY	0	0	0	0	0
TOTAL	35	43	163	169	163

Appendix - Direct US Manufacturing Jobs Generated by Exports to Comoros (By Industry)

Jobs Generated	2001	2002	2003	2004	2005
311 Processed Foods	0	0	0	0	0
312 Beverage & Tobacco Products	0	0	0	0	0
313 Fabric Mill Products	0	0	0	0	0
314 Non-Apparel Textile Products	0	0	0	0	0
315 Apparel Manufactures	0	0	0	0	0
316 Leather & Related Products	0	0	0	0	0
321 Wood Products	0	0	0	0	0
322 Paper Products	0	0	0	0	0
323 Printing & Related Products	0	0	0	0	0
324 Petroleum & Coal Products	0	0	0	0	0
325 Chemical Manufactures	0	0	0	0	0
326 Plastic & Rubber Products	0	0	0	0	0
327 Non-Metallic Mineral Mfgs.	0	0	0	0	0
331 Primary Metal Manufactures	0	0	0	0	0
332 Fabricated Metal Products	0	0	0	0	0
333 Machinery Manufactures	0	0	0	0	0
334 Computers & Electronic Prod.	3	0	0	0	0
335 Elec. Eq., Appliances & Parts	0	0	0	0	0
336 Transportation Equipment	0	0	0	0	0
337 Furniture & Related Products	0	0	0	0	0
339 Misc. Manufactures	0	0	0	0	0
Total	3	0	0	0	1

Appendix - Direct US Manufacturing Jobs Generated by Exports to Comoros (By Origin of Movement)

	2001	2002	2003	2004	2005
AL	0	0	0	0	0
AK	0	0	0	0	0
AZ	0	0	0	0	0
AR	0	0	0	0	0
CA	3	0	0	0	0
CO	0	0	0	0	0
CT	0	0	0	0	0
DE	0	0	0	0	0
DC	0	0	0	0	0
FL	0	0	0	0	0
GA	0	0	0	0	0
HI	0	0	0	0	0
ID	0	0	0	0	0
IL	0	0	0	0	0
IN	0	0	0	0	0
IA	0	0	0	0	0
KS	0	0	0	0	0
KY	0	0	0	0	0
LA	0	0	0	0	0
ME	0	0	0	0	0
MD	0	0	0	0	0
MA	0	0	0	0	0
MI	0	0	0	0	0
MN	0	0	0	0	0
MS	0	0	0	0	0
MO	0	0	0	0	0
MT	0	0	0	0	0
NE	0	0	0	0	0
NV	0	0	0	0	0

NH	0	0	0	0	0
NJ	0	0	0	0	0
NM	0	0	0	0	0
NY	0	0	0	0	0
NC	0	0	0	0	0
ND	0	0	0	0	0
OH	0	0	0	0	0
OK	0	0	0	0	0
OR	0	0	0	0	0
PA	0	0	0	0	0
RI	0	0	0	0	0
SC	0	0	0	0	0
SD	0	0	0	0	0
TN	0	0	0	0	0
TX	0	0	0	0	0
UT	0	0	0	0	0
VT	0	0	0	0	0
VA	0	0	0	0	0
WA	0	0	0	0	0
WV	0	0	0	0	0
WI	0	0	0	0	0
WY	0	0	0	0	0
TOTAL	3	0	0	0	1

Appendix - Direct and Indirect US Jobs Generated by Manufactures Exports to Comoros (By Origin of Movement)

	2001	2002	2003	2004	2005
AL	0	0	0	0	0
AK	0	0	0	0	0
AZ	0	0	0	0	0
AR	0	0	0	0	0
CA	10	0	0	0	0
CO	0	0	0	0	0
CT	0	0	0	0	0
DE	0	0	0	0	0
DC	0	0	0	0	0
FL	1	0	0	0	1
GA	0	0	0	0	0
HI	0	0	0	0	0
ID	0	0	0	0	0
IL	0	0	0	0	0
IN	0	0	0	0	0
IA	0	0	0	0	0
KS	0	0	0	0	0
KY	0	0	0	0	0
LA	0	0	0	0	0
ME	0	0	0	0	0
MD	0	0	0	0	0
MA	0	0	0	0	1
MI	0	0	0	0	0
MN	0	0	0	0	0
MS	0	0	0	0	0
MO	0	0	0	0	0
MT	0	0	0	0	0
NE	0	0	0	0	0
NV	0	0	0	0	0

NH	0	0	0	0	0
NJ	0	0	0	0	0
NM	0	0	0	0	0
NY	0	0	0	0	0
NC	0	0	0	0	0
ND	0	0	0	0	0
OH	0	0	0	0	0
OK	0	0	0	0	0
OR	0	0	0	0	0
PA	0	0	0	0	0
RI	0	0	0	0	0
SC	0	0	0	0	0
SD	0	0	0	0	0
TN	0	0	0	0	0
TX	0	0	0	0	0
UT	0	0	0	0	0
VT	0	0	0	0	0
VA	0	0	0	0	0
WA	0	0	0	0	0
WV	0	0	0	0	0
WI	0	0	0	0	0
WY	0	0	0	0	0
TOTAL	10	1	0	1	2

US Nonimmigrant Visas and Classifications[34]

Visa	Classification
	Foreign Government Officials
A-1	Ambassador, public minister, career, diplomatic or consular officer, and members of immediate family.
A-2	Other foreign government official or employee, and members of immediate family.
A-3	Attendant, servant, or personal employee of A-1 and A-2, and members of immediate family.
	Visitors
B-1	Temporary visitor for business
B-2	Temporary visitor for pleasure
	Visa Waiver Program
	Aliens in Transit
C-1	Alien in transit directly through U.S.
C-1D	Combined transit and crewman visa
C-2	Alien in transit to UN headquarters district under Section 11.(3), (4), or (5) of the Headquarters Agreement
C-3	Foreign government official, members of immediate family, attendant, servant, or personal employee, in transit
C-4	Transit without Visa, see TWOV
	Crewmen
D-1	Crewmember departing on same vessel of arrival
D-2	Crewmember departing by means other than vessel of arrival
	Treaty Traders and Treaty Investors
E-1	Treaty Trader, spouse and children
E-2	Treaty Investor, spouse and children

---

[34] US Citizenship and Immigration Services http://www.uscis.gov/graphics/services/visas.htm

	Academic Students	
F-1	Academic Student	
F-2	Spouse or child of F-1	
	For Foreign Medical Graduates (see individual categories H-1B, J-1, O-1, TN, E-2)	
	Foreign Government Officials to International Organizations	
G-1	Principal resident representative of recognized foreign member government to international organization, and members of immediate family.	
G-2	Other representative of recognized foreign member government to international organization, and members of immediate family.	
G-3	Representative of non-recognized or nonmember government to international organization, and members of immediate family	
G-4	International organization officer or employee, and members of immediate family	
G-5	Attendant, servant, or personal employee of G-1, G-2, G-3, G-4, or members of immediate family	
	Temporary Workers	
H-1B	Specialty Occupations, DOD workers, fashion models	
H-1C	Nurses going to work for up to three years in health professional shortage areas	
H-2A	Temporary Agricultural Worker	
H-2B	Temporary worker: skilled and unskilled	
H-3	Trainee	
H-4	Spouse or child of H-1, H-2, H-3	
	Foreign Media Representatives	
I	Visas for foreign media representatives	
	Exchange Visitors	
J-1	Visas for exchange visitors	
J-2	Spouse or child of J-1	
	Fiancé(e) of US Citizen	
K-1	Fiancé(e)	

K-2	Minor child of K-1
K-3	Spouse of a U.S. Citizen (LIFE Act)
K-4	Child of K-3 (LIFE Act)
	Intracompany Transferee
L-1A	Executive, managerial
L-1B	Specialized knowledge
L-2	Spouse or child of L-1
	Vocational and Language Students
M-1	Vocational student or other nonacademic student
M-2	Spouse or child of M-1
N-8	Parent of alien classified SK-3 "Special Immigrant"
N-9	Child of N-8, SK-1, SK-2, or SK-4 "Special Immigrant"
NAFTA	*North American Free Trade Agreement (NAFTA)* (see TN, below)
	North Atlantic Treaty Organization
NATO-1	Principal Permanent Representative of Member State to NATO and resident members of official staff or immediate family
NATO-2	Other representatives of member State; Dependents of Member of a Force entering in accordance with the provisions of NATO Status-of-Forces agreement; Members of such a Force if issued visas
NATO-3	Official clerical staff accompanying Representative of Member State to NATO or immediate family
NATO-4	Official of NATO other than those qualified as NATO-1 and immediate family
NATO-5	Expert other than NATO officials qualified under NATO-4, employed on behalf of NATO and immediate family
NATO-6	Member of civilian component who is either accompanying a Force entering in accordance with the provisions of the NATO Status-of-Forces agreement; attached to an Allied headquarters under the protocol on the Status of International Military headquarters set up pursuant to the North Atlantic Treaty; and their dependents
NATO-7	Servant or personal employee of NATO-1, NATO-2, NATO-3, NATO-4, NATO-5, NATO-6, or immediate family

	Workers with Extraordinary Abilities
O-1	Extraordinary ability in Sciences, Arts, Education, Business, or Athletics
O-2	Alien's (support) accompanying O-1
O-3	Spouse or child of O-1 or O-2
	Athletes and Entertainers
P-1	Individual or team athletes
P-1	Entertainment groups
P-2	Artists and entertainers in reciprocal Exchange programs
P-3	Artists and entertainers in culturally unique programs
P-4	Spouse or child of P-1, 2, or 3
	International Cultural Exchange Visitors
Q-1	International cultural exchange visitors
Q-2	Irish Peace Process Cultural and Training Program (Walsh Visas)
Q-3	Spouse or child of Q-2
	Religious Workers
R-1	Religious workers
R-2	Spouse or child of R-1
	Witness or Informant
S-5	Informant of criminal organization information
S-6	Informant of terrorism information
T	*Victims of a Severe Form of Trafficking in Persons*
T-1	Victim of a severe form of trafficking in persons
T-2	Spouse of a victim of a severe form of trafficking in persons
T-3	Child of victim of a severe form of trafficking in persons
T-4	Parent of victim of a severe form of trafficking in persons (if T-1 victim is under 21 years of age)

	North American Free Trade Agreement (NAFTA)
TN	Trade visas for Canadians and Mexicans
TD	Spouse or child accompanying TN-
	Transit Without Visa
TWOV	Passenger
TWOV	Crew
U	*Victims of Certain Crimes*
U-1	Victim of Certain Criminal Activity
U-2	Spouse of U-1
U-3	Child of U-1
U-4	Parent of U-1, if U-1 is under 21 years of age
	*Certain **Second Preference** Beneficiaries*
V-1	Spouse of an LPR who is the principal beneficiary of a family-based petition (Form I-130) which was filed prior to December 21, 2000, and has been pending for at least three years
V-2	Child of an LPR who is the principal beneficiary of a family-based visa petition (Form I-130) that was filed prior to December 21, 2000, and has been pending for at least three years.
V-3	The derivative child of a V-1 or V-2
	Humanitarian Parole
	Temporary Protected Status (TPS)
TPS	Temporary Protected Status

Appendix: Status of WTO and Bilateral U.S.-Arab Free Trade Agreements

"The United States has been working with Saudi Arabia for over a decade on its Membership bid. The negotiations have been tough given the complexity of the issues. Trade Minister Yamani and his team have worked hard to pursue real economic reforms that will contribute to peace and stability in the region." U.S. Trade Representative Robert Portman 9/9/2005

The successful conclusion of US-Saudi talks for the Kingdom's membership in the World Trade Organization on September 9, 2005 is an important milestone. A review of the Arab market reveals that most states are now full members of the WTO with attendant rights to shape the global trade environment at top level negotiations such as the Doha Round. Arab state membership in the World Trade Organization has been a catalyst for increased trade and bilateral negotiations with the U.S. Trade Representative (USTR). WTO dispute mechanisms allow members to confront external trade barriers even while pushing through needed but unpopular domestic reforms. The new USTR recently called for more proactive WTO membership and compromise toward concluding successful global trade talks talking place in Hong Kong in December of 2005.

'We are at the point where we can no longer procrastinate and hope for the best in Hong Kong,' 'Agriculture is the key to unblocking the blockages in the Doha round,' - Robert Portman September 8, 2005.

WTO membership has normally been a precursor to negotiating any bilateral Free Trade Agreement (FTA) with the U.S. Bilateral investment treaties (BITs) are more comprehensive agreements delineating reciprocity in the promotion and protection of investments in each state's territories by corporations. The BITS signed between the U.S. and Arab market states cover dispute resolution mechanisms, definition of investment, and treatment, and investments between corporations of each party state.

Current Status of Arab Market WTO Membership, BITs, TIFAs and FTAs

(Sources: World Trade Organization and the U.S. Trade Representative)

Country	WTO Membership	BIT	TIFA	FTA
Algeria	Observer, requested ascension in 1987		2001	
Bahrain	1995	2001	2002	2004 signed, ratified
Comoros				
Djibouti	1995			
Egypt	1995	1992	1999	Official candidate
Iraq	Observer, requested ascension in 2004		2005	
Jordan	2000	2003	1999	2000 signed, ratified, effective 1/1/2006
Kuwait	1995		2004	Unofficial candidate
Lebanon	Observer, requested ascension in 1999, probable 2006			
Libya	Observer, requested ascension in 2004			
Morocco	1995	1991	1995	2004 signed, ratified
Oman	2000		2004	2005 signed, 2006 ratified
Qatar	1996		2004	Unofficial candidate
Saudi Arabia	2005		2003	
Sudan	Observer, requested ascension in 1994			
Tunisia	1995	1993	2002	
United Arab Emirates	1996		2004	2005 under negotiation
Yemen	Observer, requested ascension in 2000		2004	

Judging the pace of signing U.S. Trade Investment Framework Agreements (TIFAs), Bilateral Investment Treaties, and Free Trade Agreements (FTAs) with the Arab market is a matter of perception. Optimists will point out that four of the U.S. free trade agreements ratified by Congress are Arab market states. Pessimists lament that while 80% of the Arab market's import potential is covered by TIFAs, less than 20% of import demand potential can be tapped by U.S. exporters under the FTA umbrella.

The number of TIFAs signed between the U.S. and Arab market countries reveal their non-binding and relatively uncomplicated framework for creating an "open and predictable" business environment. Most TIFAs are four page documents establishing a consultative framework to discuss investment and trade. TIFAs are considered by the USTR to be a critical milestone between WTO membership which initially opens economies to international trade and investment, and a comprehensive and binding bilateral U.S. Free Trade Agreement. Unfortunately, according to a recent study by the GAO, U.S. infrastructure and resources for negotiating and signing many comprehensive FTAs simultaneously simply doesn't exist.

The major constraint is not funding according to a study of the USTR conducted by the Government Accountability Office (GAO). The USTR's total cost to negotiate an Arab market FTAs has been minimal, especially considering the enormous benefits. Steps toward negotiations and signing an FTA cost roughly the same amount whether the U.S. negotiating partner is an individual country or a customs union. The Morocco FTA cost USTR $339,000 while CAFTA cost $341,000 according to GAO. The main constraints against broadening the number of bilateral deals are highly specialized USTR staff resources, the partner selection and deal "sequencing". Each of the six FTAs under negotiation in the year 2003 required 11 percent of USTR's 209 full-time staff members. Demands on other agencies are also high. FTA negotiations also require intensive effort on the part of agencies such as Commerce, Agriculture, Treasury, and the State Department.

The GAO believes that resource constraints have meant that negotiations in a given region have been stacked into a "start to finish" production line, with little multitasking. According to GAO, although Bahrain was ready to begin negotiating immediately with the United States in 2002, the USTR's Office of Europe and the Mediterranean postponed negotiations until the completion of the Morocco FTA.

The opportunity costs of backlogged FTAs in the Arab market are tangible to U.S. exporters. U.S. exports to Jordan grew on average 0.33% annually in the five year period preceding the FTA. The five years after the FTA produced average annual export increases of 14.98%. The addition of the Jordan FTA helped boost U.S. exports by an additional U.S. $713 million since the year 2000.

U.S. Merchandise Exports to Jordan –Five Years Before and After 2000 FTA
(Source: U.S. Census Division Foreign Trade Division)

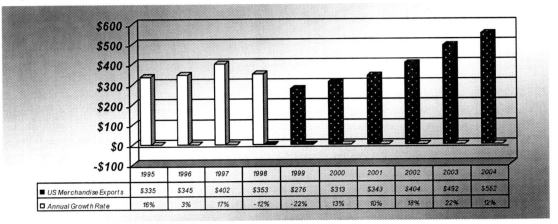

	1995	1996	1997	1998	1999	2000	2001	2002	2003	2004
US Merchandise Exports	$335	$345	$402	$353	$276	$313	$343	$404	$492	$552
Annual Growth Rate	16%	3%	17%	-12%	-22%	13%	10%	18%	22%	12%

America wasn't the only winner. Five year pre-FTA Jordanian exports to the U.S. grew on average eight percent per year. After the deal Jordanian exports growth exploded to 111% annually reaching just under $1.1 billion in the year 2004. However, while the benefits may be uncontroversial, FTA negotiations aren't always free of conflict.

Some sticking points in U.S. FTA negotiations are the product of cultural perceptions and even myopia. Non-citizen guest workers are under heavy restrictions with respect to labor organization, yet millions of foreigners pour into the Gulf for economic opportunities. Compared to the millions of illegal immigrant workers in the U.S., some believe Gulf worker status and rights are actually more transparent than U.S. labor laws and enforcement regarding illegal alien workers. Never the less, non-citizen labor rules have been an issue raised by the U.S. in recent FTA negotiations.

U.S. negotiating priorities raise the larger issue of the partner selection process. In January 2005, the National Association of Manufacturers advocated FTA negotiations with Egypt, South Korea, Malaysia, New Zealand, and India on primarily economic grounds. Some have complained that longstanding and even misguided U.S. Middle East foreign policy objectives have played too strong a role structuring the FTA pipeline and that economic benefits from bilateral deals with countries or customs unions must be an end in themselves. The USTR believes that readiness levels of FTA aspirants in the region in many cases is too low.

"Internal resources and scheduling are not as big an issue or delay as partner readiness levels. Many states need to make significant internal adjustments before we can begin to negotiate an FTA that can be passed by Congress and successfully implemented" says Jason Buntin of the U.S. Trade Representative's office covering the Middle East. "While economically a deal might make sense, there are delays when partner countries don't resolve adjustment issues." USTR also concedes that foreign policy matters a great deal: "An FTA is the highest level of economic engagement between the U.S. and another country," said Bill Jackson of the USTR Africa group, "clearly we're not going to enter into an agreement with a state with which we have major policy differences." The economic potential of more FTAs from a regional standpoint are immense.

Executive branch officials hope that Morocco will become a hub for sub regional integration and later become integrated into the Middle East Free Trade Area (MEFTA) envisioned by President Bush.

> "The Arab World has a great cultural tradition, but is largely missing out on the economic progress of our time," President Bush said at the University of South Carolina in May 2003. "So I propose the establishment of a U.S.-Middle East Free Trade Area within a decade, to bring the Middle East into an expanding circle of opportunity, to provide hope for the people who live in that region."

The MEFTA is the guiding vision for USTR negotiations. However larger questions remain as to whether a bilateral FTA with Bahrain, an important but minor member of the Gulf Cooperation Council (GCC) customs union composed of Kuwait, Oman, Qatar, Saudi Arabia and United Arab Emirates, is a short cut or added delay toward a deeper U.S.-GCC trade relations or reaching the 2013 MEFTA vision.

The U.S. is not alone in recognizing the social and economic benefits of comprehensive trade deals with the Arab market. In 1989 the GCC and the European Commission executed a Cooperative Agreement with a commitment from both sides to enter into FTA negotiations. The two are actively pursuing more intensive FTA talks even as U.S. merchandise and service exporters jockey for a better position to serve surging Arab markets. Efficiently working through an attractive lineup negotiating partners and initiating parallel accelerated FTA negotiations should become a major USTR priority in 2007.

Appendix: Saudi Executive Interviews - Nabeel Al Mojil

1. How much has travel to the US changed since 9/11?

I haven't been to the US since 9/11 and it will also be my last option to travel unless it is mandatory or when 9/11 negative impacts begin to fade away.

2. How has the process for acquiring a US B-1 (business) or B-2 (tourist) changed? Is there relative parity in the difficulty of US visitors entering Saudi Arabia for business and tourism?

Well, in the past the US embassy processed our visa requests with the minimum paper required and remotely too. Now and according to everyone I know whether he/she is going on business or pleasure, it is very hectic and in most cases they have to come in person. Just imagine what people living in the Northern or southern region go through (limited air flights or dangerous long roads to drive). On the other hand, I haven't heard that US visitors entering KSA have had more difficulty since 9/11. Meaning it hasn't changed.

3. What non-visa issues affect Saudis decision process for traveling to the US? What negative factors are now considered?

Some people got a feeling that Saudis are no longer welcome to enter the US anymore. Also the recent verdict against Mr. Hamdan Al Turki made Saudis confused and raised a lot of concerns about the USA justice impartiality and independence.

4. Is the US losing business, in your opinion, for visa, and non-visa related travel restrictions? Is the US national security enhanced by the current level of restrictions?

If a university loses a foreign student that decides to choose other places then it is a loss to the US. If a US company can not make a deal with Saudis due to visa problems then the country is also losing. Every penny counts. The US national security did enhance in airports but not sure in its citizen's heart.

5. What does the US need to do to return to pre-9/11 Saudi visitor flow of businesspeople, students and tourists?

Continue to be on alert status but not too paranoid. Some people got a feeling that we are no longer welcome to enter the US anymore.

6. What is at stake for the future if the present level of visa hurdles remain?

Well, maybe our business will shift to Europe, China and Far East in general. We will pick up new languages). When you knock my door several times (looking for business or providing one) and no one is answering the door in a reasonable time, you tend to go somewhere else.

7. How much did you travel to the US before 9/11? After? How has your personal travel been changed, if at all?

Before 9/11 around 2 times a year, after 9/11 as I said in answer # 1 NONE (why do I have to go through unnecessary hassle?) But maybe next year when my son graduates from high school. I will contact a few universities in my home town Portland Oregon and see how it goes. I still have faith on the USA I know, not the current one!!

Thanks for giving me this opportunity.

My Best Regards

Nabeel Al Mojil
Dammam, Saudi Arabia

Appendix: Saudi Executive Interviews - Mohammed al-Misehal

1. How much has travel to the US changed since 9/11?

It has changed a lot! Before 9/11 I used to wish to travel to the US every year. After 9/11, I wish I don't have to!

2. How has the process for acquiring a US B-1 (business) or B-2 (tourist) changed? Is there relative parity in the difficulty of US visitors entering Saudi Arabia for business and tourism?

The process has a dramatic negative change after 9/11. When visa processing takes less than 24 hours to be processed (at the US consulate in Dhahran) before 9/11, takes now more than 2 to 3 weeks in normal cases, and 2 to 3 months in other cases (In Riyadh Embassy)! Then yes, there is a change! Provided that when a family applies for a tourism visa before 9/11, they'll never be surprised by rejecting a child and his mom, and at the same time for the same application, accepting a teen age boy and his father of the same family for the entry visa! I see this as an inconsistent mess. With my respect of course!

3. What non-visa issues affect Saudis decision process for traveling to the US? What negative factors are now considered?

The US government has given its ....media to convince the majority of the US citizens with loads and loads of fake stories and myths about the Muslims in General and Saudis in particular. Also, we hear from many friends, the experiences they've went through in the US airports as soon as they reach the immigration desk. They treat many of them like if they were criminals! Why would I subject my self for all this hassle? Why would I subject my self to be verbally or especially harmed in the street or being indirectly or directly humiliated and insulted in the immigration office or by the FBI?! It's not worth it!

4. Is the US losing business, in your opinion, for visa, and non-visa related travel restrictions? Is the US national security enhanced by the current level of restrictions?

Yes, the US business has been harmed of course, due to the visa and non-visa restrictions for obvious reasons. But I don't think that the US national security has been enhanced by the current level of restrictions! If any of the US enemies would like to come up with a terrorist mission against the US, all these enhancements will be taken in consideration! For the US to have a very sealed security mechanism for it's nation, is simply by going back to the principals of George

Washington, that was based on trading with other nations, avoid interfering in their internal issues and never create wars or support invaders! George W Bush is exactly doing the same. Therefore, it is obvious that since George Washington's time up to the day before GWB wins 50.001% of the US elections votes, the US hasn't ever been under such threat, and hasn't ever been hated by other nations like it is now!

5. What does the US need to do to return to pre-9/11 Saudi visitor flow of businesspeople, students and tourists?

Learn and implement global Justice. And believe that freedom, human rights and dignity is also the right of other human beings living on Earth. Not only for American citizens.

6. What is at stake for the future if the present level of visa hurdles remain?

The ideological gap between the Saudi's and Americans will be enlarged, day after day. If this means anything to the Americans, then this thing is at a stake!

7. How much did you travel to the US before 9/11? After? How has your personal travel been changed, if at all?

I've been to the US three times before the 9/11. None after. My personal travel hasn't been changed. Except that the US isn't in my destination list anymore, and I really hope and wish I won't need to have back on the list again! Not even for my dependants.

Mohammed al-Misehal
Riyadh, Saudi Arabia